Foundations of Mariachi Education

VOLUME 1

Materials, Methods, and Resources

Edited by
WILLIAM GRADANTE

D1525357

Published in partnership with
MENC: The National Association for Music Education
Frances S. Ponick, Executive Editor

ROWMAN & LITTLEFIELD EDUCATION
Lanham • *New York* • *Toronto* • *Plymouth, UK*

Published in partnership with
MENC: The National Association for Music Education

Published in the United States of America
by Rowman & Littlefield Education
A Division of Rowman & Littlefield Publishers, Inc.
A wholly owned subsidary of The Rowman & Littlefield Publishing Group, Inc.
4501 Forbes Boulevard, Suite 200, Lanham, Maryland 20706
www.rowmaneducation.com

Estover Road
Plymouth PL6 7PY
United Kingdom

British Library Cataloguing in Publication Information Available

Library of Congress Cataloging-in-Publication Data

Foundations of mariachi education / edited by William Gradante.
    p. cm.
  ISBN-13: 978-1-57886-763-9 (cloth : alk. paper)
  ISBN-10: 1-57886-763-0 (cloth : alk. paper)
  ISBN-13: 978-1-57886-764-6 (pbk. : alk. paper)
  ISBN-10: 1-57886-764-9 (pbk. : alk. paper)
  1. Mariachi—Instruction and study. I. Gradante, William. II. MENC, the
National Association for Music Education (U.S.)
  MT146.F68 2008
  784.4—dc22   2007047901

©™ The paper used in this publication meets the minimum requirements of
American National Standard for Information Sciences—Permanence of Paper
for Printed Library Materials, ANSI/NISO Z39.48-1992.
Manufactured in the United States of America

Contents

Foreword

Daniel Sheehy

Mariachi music is a success story still in the making. Born of humble origins on the ranches and in the small towns of western Mexico in the nineteenth century, it was crowned a national symbol in the twentieth. Today, the sound of the mariachi stirs the emotions of performers and listeners in countries throughout the Western Hemisphere and Europe, and the silver-studded image of the mariachi instills pride in anyone who steps into the *traje de charro*, the mariachi suit. It also is a success because, parallel to blues and bluegrass in the United States, it is one of a small number of Latin American musical traditions that have found broad acceptance in the professional music industry while at the same time remaining rooted in the sentiments and identity of a unique culture.

The twentieth century brought sweeping changes to Mexican society. Rural people flocked to urban centers, Mexico City in particular. From the 1930s to the 1950s, the mariachi experienced a profound transformation, changing from a loose-knit rural ensemble performing for local social occasions into a professionalized, codified, and

romanticized ensemble that withstood the musical scrutiny of sophisticated urban audiences at the same time that it appealed to their
idealized notions of their rural roots. The music spread throughout
Mexico and beyond. Radio, cinema, recordings, and television cata-
pulted it to major international notoriety throughout the Americas.
Its repertoire expanded to include a rainbow of musical genres, each
with its distinctive effect, performance techniques, and history. The
technical mastery required in the top-tier ensembles dramatically increased, and the professional expectations and unforgiving technology of the recording studio made it inevitable that written scores and
formal musical training become a prerequisite of most successful professional musicians' careers. While workaday music groups continued
to enliven informal social events, highly skilled mariachi artists took
to the concert stages, toured abroad, and won Grammy Awards.

So what does this mean for the United States? It means that mariachi
music has been part of life in this country since the 1930s. Decades of
popular films, influential recordings, and live performances rooted it
deeply in the Mexican American community. But here, the mariachi
story diverges on the U.S. side of the border. Culture was at the core of
the Chicano movement for civil rights that emerged in the 1960s, and
Chicano leaders honored mariachi music as a cherished symbol of Mexican American identity. Cultural activists organized mariachi teaching
programs in local schools. In the 1970s and 1980s, local enthusiasts
throughout the Southwest launched major international mariachi festivals with educational workshops at their core. The number of school
programs and other instructional opportunities exploded. Studies
showed that mariachi-in-schools programs lowered the high school
dropout rate of participants and improved overall student achievement.
The increased enrollment in mariachi performance programs helped
offset the decline in overall music enrollment in some schools. The programs attracted "parent power" among Mexican American parents who
had felt alienated by language, cultural, and musical barriers, strength-
ening the school–community bond. Cultural barriers faded as non-

Mexican students gained insight into Mexican culture through playing mariachi music, and at the same time, they acquired new language skills and gained musical versatility. Not being of Mexican heritage myself, I can tell you that my experiences learning to play mariachi music as a college undergraduate in the late 1960s were among the most enlightening, enduring, and cherished of my entire educational career.

Is this the happy ending to our story? No, unfortunately. Success bred challenges. The expansion of mariachi education outpaced the ability of the system to accommodate the demand and to keep the quality of instruction high. Well-intended school administrators mandated ill-prepared music instructors to teach mariachi music. Music scores and instructional guides were either nonexistent or of varying quality. When music teachers themselves took the lead, their attempts to make the case for mariachi music fitting into curriculum standards and to gain the necessary knowledge and skills were all too often met with frustration. Opportunities for peer advice and skills development were too few and too far between. The increasing demand continued to outstrip the available skill sets and instructional resources, and teachers, administrators, and students continued to scramble to do the best they could.

Here enters MENC: The National Association for Music Education and its Mariachi Advisory Committee. The committee, formalized at the national conference in 2006, wasted no time in addressing these critical issues. It launched a monthly *Mariachi Newsletter* featuring strategically selected articles by seasoned mariachi educators on a panorama of mariachi education topics, aiming to instill greater academic rigor, solid pedagogy, and core fundamentals and repertoire in mariachi education. The how-to articles honed in on the instruction of the mariachi instruments and singing style, practical considerations in starting a program, and finding instructional resources. This book is the compilation of this breakthrough effort and deserves a standing ovation, along with many Mexican-style *gritos* (shouts) of joy and encouragement: ¡*ajúa*! It is a giant step in closing the gap between the dream and the reality of excellence in mariachi education.

Dr. Daniel Sheehy is the director and curator of Smithsonian Folkways Recordings and Smithsonian Global Sound, the nonprofit record label and digital music Web site for the national museum. He served as coeditor of the South America, Mexico, Central America, and the Caribbean *volume of the* Garland Encyclopedia of World Music *and authored* Mariachi Music in America: Experiencing Music, Expressing Culture. *He has performed mariachi music for forty years.*

Introduction

William Gradante

Our MENC National Advisory Committee for Mariachi Education was put together with the conscious desire to include not only mariachi educators or performers representing various regions across the country but also individuals whose collective experience and areas of expertise varied widely. Thus, among the authors of the present volume, we find full-time teachers, educational administrators, and top-flight professional performers and recording artists. Several have, to one degree or another, participated in both the teaching and performing aspects during their careers. Within this multicolored tapestry that is the collective experience of our authorship, however, there run certain common threads that tie this entire volume together.

First, I detect a great deal of pride in the recent surge in the nationwide recognition of the accomplishments of our mariachi students and educators. As Daniel Sheehy (2006) points out in his recent study, *Mariachi Music in America*, tens of thousands of students are currently enrolled in hundreds of school mariachi classes across the nation. This has to be regarded as an enormous achievement when one takes into consideration the dire lack of *certified* teachers working to weave appropriate mariachi elements into existing public school music curricula. In light of the fact that the cultural and educational value of mariachi music education is just beginning to be discovered and appreciated, these are encouraging accomplishments. Unfortunately, the smooth transition from professional performer to credentialed mariachi educator, as described in our case study of Clark County, Nevada, is the exception to the rule, but it definitely gives us cause for optimism!

Second, because such an august body as MENC has now recognized mariachi education as a highly desirable and endorsed area of study, the authors evince a clear sense of pride that we as long-time proponents of mariachi education have at last arrived. This, of course, comes with serious challenges. If we are to be treated as fully respected partners in the business of music education, we must organize our pedagogical goals and performance expectations within formal curricula, reflecting the academic rigor our individual mariachi programs require in our quest for student excellence. The six chapters devoted to teaching *guitarrón*, *armonías*, violin, trumpet, harp, and voice represent seminal efforts in that direction.

Now is the time for mariachi education to come of age. Although we have graduated several generations of mariachi students, it is disappointing that only a limited number have expressed an interest in following us into the ranks of educators who value mariachi music education. Thus, while many of my own students have gone on to careers in the performing arena, few have ever seriously considered becoming certified music teachers able to step into our positions as we retire or to establish new programs of their own. There is good money to be earned—and glamour to be enjoyed—performing as a mariachi, whereas, in my district at least, the only way to secure a position as a mariachi teacher is to first get a job as a certified band director. This is clearly a deterrent.

In our district, students can participate in mariachi music programs in eight middle or high schools. Myself excepted, every mariachi teacher in the district is a band or orchestra director who has *never performed in a mariachi ensemble* and who has absolutely no formal training in mariachi education. It is almost unfathomable, on the other hand, that a local band director was not himself or herself a "band nerd" back in middle school, high school, and college. Well, now is the time for the "mariachi nerds" to stand up and be counted—the coming generations need you to become certified mariachi educators!

Third, all of us have met teachers who have been assigned the position of mariachi teacher, in spite of their acknowledged lack of preparation in the field. Such positions often come into being as the result of student and community pressure to establish a mariachi program in their schools. These individuals show up at MENC meetings and mariachi conferences, contact us at the MENC Mariachi Web page, and even visit our classrooms to pick our brains, asking things like

- "How do I begin?"
- "How do I get the administration to implement/support a mariachi program?"
- "What kind of budget will I need?"
- "What kind of budget can I actually expect?"
- "Should the class be offered before, during, or after school?"
- "What is acceptable instrumentation?"
- "Should classes feature homogenous or heterogeneous instrumentation?"
- "Where do I get sheet music/uniforms/instruments?"
- "What should my curriculum look like?"
- "Which are the 'good' mariachis and singers to listen to?"
- "Where can I get advice on repertoire?"
- "How should I arrange students onstage?"
- "What kind of guitars should we buy?"
- "How is a *guitarrón* tuned?"
- "Is the mariachi violin played like the regular violin?"
- "Is the band director correct in claiming that playing in the mariachi group will ruin his first trumpeter's embouchure for 'band music?'"
- and so on and so forth.

The purpose of this book is to systematically respond to these questions and to pose and provide answers to many more. This is exciting for us, and we authors are happy to be resources. Please feel free to contact us by visiting the mariachi forum at www.menc.org/mariachi or by e-mailing us (contact information is also available at www.menc.org/mariachi). We relish the opportunity to share the experience we have gleaned through our many years in the field, help you avoid making the same kinds of mistakes we have made, and subsequently hear your success stories. Again, we come from different parts of the country; have different cultural, socioeconomic, and educational backgrounds; and have different primary instruments. This is intentional, as it creates a broad scope of input. Since each of our personal philosophies and current teaching situations is inherently different from everyone else's, there's a good chance that the reality of mariachi education for at least one of us may to some degree coincide with your own.

Fourth, this book also directs its attention toward those teachers who find themselves in established mariachi programs. In *Mariachi Music in America*, Sheehy (2006) presents excerpts from multiple interviews with the directors of today's top professional mariachi ensembles, including Nati Cano of Mariachi Los Camperos, Randy and Steve Carrillo of Mariachi Cobre, José Hernández of Mariachi Sol de México, and Pepe Martínez of Mariachi Vargas de Tecalitlán. The interviews display an undercurrent of uneasiness at the current direction of mariachi education, the suspicion that things may, in fact, be moving along too rapidly.

At the heart of this is the concern that, although the technical competence of today's mariachi students is dramatically increasing, they still may not be receiving the kind of training that will ultimately prepare them for performance at the highest levels. Among other things, we instructors may be placing too much emphasis on teaching music that our students hear on the latest commercial recordings *and that they optimistically assume they can adequately imitate.* More class time spent developing the solid instrumental and vocal technique required to perform such pieces—*in the future, after graduation*—is clearly preferable to concentrating on current mariachi fads, gimmick pieces, or music that students cannot yet perform successfully.

Thus, we must place greater emphasis upon guiding our students toward a more thorough acquaintance with and mastery of more standard mariachi repertoire. (A sample list of mariachi standards, compiled from titles suggested by the MENC Mariachi Advisory Committee, is presented in the appendix.) This should be considered absolutely essential and is an area in which a conscientiously organized mariachi curriculum must be fundamentally different from the curricula guiding band, choir, and orchestra programs.

No one has any problem with a high school marching band performing an eight-minute halftime program consisting of a medley of television show theme music. Toward what kind of standard band repertoire must the high school director be made to feel responsible? Should performance of these pieces be made mandatory for band students across the school district? Of course not! In the same vein, a middle school choir's spring concert may well be comprised of a number of popular movie themes performed with snappy dance steps and cute costumes.

Mariachi is different. When the mariachi takes the stage, its costume—the traditional *traje de mariachi* or *traje de charro*—carries with it over a century of profound historical meaning. Our students shoulder a sociocultural responsibility not to be taken lightly, that of proudly representing not only their family, class, school, and community but also a time-honored tradition of an entire culture. When the mariachi performs selections from the standard repertoire, such as "La Negra," "Ay, Jalisco, No Te Rajes," "El Rey," or "Cucurrucucú Paloma," it taps into a belief system and shared cultural heritage that have ramifications extending well beyond the walls of the school auditorium and long after the spotlights go out.

Finally, I would like to thank the authors of the chapters that follow for taking the time to share their lifelong experience in both performing mariachi music and teaching our young people to love it as much as we do. Although we are not professional writers, we have done our best to pass on this intense affinity for mariachi music and mariachi education to teachers, students, and *future teachers of mariachi music.* Above all, we share a passionate desire to see mariachi music education become both more systematically rigorous and widely available to our young people. I think I can safely say that we yearn for the same status as the band program—both in artistic respect and in budgetary matters. In order to prove ourselves worthy of the elevated status that MENC has conferred upon us, it must become our mission to renew our own efforts to provide quality mariachi programs and simultaneously encourage and assist the new generation of mariachi educators as they move with us into the future.

REFERENCE

Sheehy, D. (2006). *Mariachi music in America.* New York: Oxford University Press.

1

Starting a Mariachi Program

Noé Sánchez

Schools all around the country are making the decisive move to start mariachi programs for their students. They realize that mariachi music not only reaches more Hispanic students than traditional music classes, but it also offers non-Hispanic students a broader cultural base. Perhaps the biggest challenge for schools wanting to start a mariachi program is the program's implementation. To accomplish this task successfully, several steps need to be taken.

1. CREATE A PROPOSAL FOR YOUR PRINCIPAL OR ADMINISTRATION

Decision makers need to have facts and figures to plan ahead. You need to turn in your proposal six months to a year before your planned start to allow administrators time to consider it. The proposal should include instructors necessary to teach the class, number of students expected, schedule, a budget to purchase instruments, classroom space requirements, and such resources as music and strings. Uniforms should not be included until the students can play a few songs. Talk to other mariachi directors in your area, or attend a mariachi conference to acquire information for planning your program. Also refer to chapter 11 for potential problems and issues to anticipate.

1

2. SELECT AN INSTRUCTOR

Not having a dedicated instructor jeopardizes all your hard work in starting a program. Once the principal has approved your proposal, then immediately start advertising for the position. Know how much this position pays and how many classes are offered. Begin interviewing applicants as soon as possible. You want to hire an instructor who is qualified in teaching mariachi music. That means that this person should have a pedagogy background in class management and teaching processes. This person should be knowledgeable in mariachi repertoire and mariachi instruments. Places to look for qualified applicants are:

- university music departments
- mariachi conferences
- other school mariachi programs, and
- local talent.

3. SECURE A ROOM

A room is essential for the mariachi classes. Your mariachi program will be more successful if the mariachi students feel that their program is respected as much as the other music programs. A separate room dedicated to mariachi instruction works best if at all possible. The room should be equipped with storage for mariachi instruments; a stereo; a piano; a chalkboard with staff lines; practice rooms; and an office to store music, strings, and the other items you need for your program.

4. SCHEDULE YOUR CLASSES

Since beginner students learn best in homogeneous classes, work with only one instrument type at a time, grouping violins, trumpets, *armonías* (guitars, *vihuelas*), and so on. After students have perfected musical fundamentals, combine them into heterogeneous classes. It might be possible to schedule some rehearsals after school or during the day to combine the students into groups. You need to recruit early to ensure that you have students to cover each instrument. If possible, have an established mariachi group perform at your elementary and middle-level feeder schools to demonstrate each of the traditional mariachi instruments.

5. DEVELOP A CURRICULUM

Start by visiting the MENC Web site (www.menc.org/mariachi), and view the various mariachi curricula listed. These examples provide a good foundation to develop what works best for your school and students. The MENC Web site also provides resources vital to your new mariachi program's development. Use the mariachi forum to ask fellow MENC members about teaching mariachi instruments and repertoire.

6. PURCHASE INSTRUMENTS

Your next step is to start purchasing instruments. It is wise to submit purchase orders before or during May so you have instruments in the students' hands when school starts. The Mariachi Connection (www.mariachiconnection.com) is the largest distributor of mariachi supplies in the country and can provide the instruments, sheet music, strings, uniforms, and accessories you need for your program. To find other reliable sources for mariachi supplies, contact fellow directors of mariachi programs, and ask for their recommendations. Consult with your school bookkeeper to see if bids are necessary for purchase orders over a certain amount. Remember to plan all of this well in advance of your needs.

7. TEACH THE CLASS

Plan to provide staff development or curriculum guidance to the instructor you hire, especially if that individual does not have a university degree, and make sure to gear staff development specifically to mariachi. It is vital that the instructor understand all school policies and procedures. If you hire a band, orchestra, or choir director to teach the mariachi class, consider purchasing instructional videos to help your instructor become more proficient on less familiar instruments.

Once your teacher is in place, have that person create a "scope and sequence" for the program. Have that teacher use the curriculum developed with the help of MENC resources, write up detailed lesson plans, and start implementing those lesson plans from the beginning. Remember, this *is* a music class teaching music fundamentals. Your teacher is simply doing so using the vehicle of mariachi music and tapping into the cultural history of your students.

I hope the pointers provided help you to start and implement a mariachi program at your school. I recommend that you start your planning early, use the expertise of those already in the field to help you build your program, and bring this beautiful music to as broad a student population as possible. You will be amazed at the student participation, the community support, and the parent involvement a program like this can provide to your school and music department.

2

Starting the Year

Noé Sánchez

The previous chapter introduced us to starting a mariachi program by providing a basic framework for directors interested in implementing a program. Once everything is in place, though, how do you get started? The first step is to schedule the students into the appropriate mariachi class section. This will let you know how many students you have. Confirm that your school has the necessary instruments. If not, start creating purchase orders with bids so you can order instruments for your students.

Over the first five years of teaching, I realized I was repeating some mistakes. To remedy this, I decided to create a "How to Start the School Year" folder. In this folder, I placed all my vital information to begin the school year. Here are examples of items I placed in this folder.

CLASS SYLLABUS

I created my class syllabus so that the students and I would understand what I was going to cover throughout the year. In the syllabus, I included all my expectations, rules, grading procedures, and class routine, as well as supplies students needed to buy, such as a three-ring binder for their music, pencils, manuscript paper, and other class materials.

HANDBOOK

I created a mariachi handbook in which I went into great detail about concerts, procedures, performance attire, expectations, rules, and consequences of not following procedures; I also included a generic permission slip for all performances and a document for parents and students to sign as an official contract in order to participate in the program. Have your handbook approved by your administration before passing it out to students. If a dispute with a student arises, you will be able to count on the support of the administration since the parents and students both signed the mariachi contract. Some sample handbook materials have been included in this chapter, but as every school district will have its own set of forms, the mariachi teacher should check with the administrator to acquire the appropriate permission form, medical release form, and instrument contract.

INSTRUMENT CONTRACT

All students who use a school instrument should sign an instrument contract. Include vital information in this contract, such as instrument; current condition; model; serial number; value; responsibility; and consequences for losing, breaking, or damaging the instrument. I do not let any student play an instrument until contracts and fees have been returned. If your school does not provide instruments, this step is unnecessary.

INSTRUMENT AND CLASS INVENTORY

If you establish a program from scratch, create an inventory of equipment in your assigned room, such as chairs, piano, and stereo. If you walk into an established program, ask for an updated inventory document. Create your own inventory list of available equipment, including furniture, playable instruments, and uniforms. Compare these two to make sure they match. This will help you budget for the principal and document your needs. Update your inventory document annually if your school does not do so already.

MARIACHI STUDENT INVENTORY ASSIGNMENT

On the first day of school, when you have to take care of a lot of paperwork, pass out a brief questionnaire about the class. Include questions such as:

1. What do you expect from this class?
2. What are you willing to do to become a better mariachi student?
3. What is your favorite song?
4. Who is your favorite mariachi group?
5. List your five favorite mariachi songs.

This assignment helps you find out your students' favorite tunes and performers and gives you a sense of their general knowledge of mariachi.

MUSIC LITERACY EXAM

Create a music literacy exam that covers fundamentals and basic concepts you would expect students to know. This test requires only written responses, but you could include listening skills as well. Give the test during the first week of class; by determining the level of music theory your students understand, this test gives you an idea of where to start.

PLAYING TEST

If you are going to an established program, provide students with a playing exam. The results help you choose repertoire at their level and plan your year. For example, you can have violins, trumpets, and *guitarrones* play scales as well as a mariachi song. Guitarists and *vihuela* players should be able to play the scales as well as have chord fingering and *mánico* (strumming) knowledge.

MARIACHI BOOSTER CLUB BYLAWS AND CONSTITUTION

Parent support is essential for a successful program. If the school does not have a booster club, create your own bylaws and constitution. Look at other programs (you can find many bylaws of different music organizations on the Internet) to give you ideas for creating your own. Submit these bylaws for administrative approval, and schedule a parent or booster club meeting as soon as possible. For more suggestions, refer to the Music Booster Manual published by MENC and available at www.rowmaneducation.com.

TRAJE (UNIFORM) FORM

If you have uniforms, make sure you sign out any items passed out to students that need to be returned to the school, such as belts, ties, and boots. Make sure students know the date by which the items must be returned and the cost for replacement if items are lost or damaged.

EQUIPMENT CHECK-IN LIST

Once you pass out all your forms, including your handbook, instrument contract, and uniform form, create a return-of-items form for each class. Use this document to check off students' names as they return each form. Place all forms in a three-ring binder to consolidate everything in one location.

LESSON PLANS FOR EVERY CLASS

Create lesson plans for every class to help you structure your curriculum. For the first few weeks of class, teach music fundamentals, listen to mariachi music, watch videos on mariachi and instrument technique, and have students play old repertoire. Once all forms have been returned and you have assigned the instruments, you can begin to teach new material. Use the class set of method books for all instruments, and have warm-ups, scales, vocal exercises, and songs already planned out.

MASTER SEATING CHART

Create a generic seating chart for your class to help you memorize your students' names.

OTHER RELEVANT FORMS

As you go through the year, develop other necessary forms as you see a need for them. Be sure to keep both electronic and hard copies, and keep backups off site.

CREATE A WEB PAGE

Create a Web page for your students and parents to visit. Provide vital information, such as rehearsals, concert dates, and booster club meetings. Include links about mariachi history, research steps, and other resources. If you have written or compiled your own material, upload it in PDF format.

I hope this information helps you get started. Keeping a "How to Start the School Year" folder has helped me immensely throughout my years of teaching. I wish someone had told me to do this a long time ago. Remember, you may add forms as your year progresses, but it is important to have some sort of contract and class structure from the beginning to be successful. Good luck this year!

SOMERSET INDEPENDENT SCHOOL DISTRICT
MARIACHI PROGRAM HANDBOOK
MR. SÁNCHEZ, MR. LÓPEZ (DIRECTORS)

Mariachi Student's Responsibilities

1. You must be present in class.
2. Be respectful to others at school and when visiting other campuses.
3. Follow all classroom rules at all times while in school and while away from campus.
4. Practice every day. You will not improve if you don't practice!

Attendance

Attendance of all mariachi events is required. This includes rehearsals and performances. All events are scheduled ahead of time, and students are responsible for transportation. The student should notify the instructor of any conflicts at least two weeks prior to the performance. Unexcused absences will reduce the student's grade. Examples of excused absences are death in the family, personal illness (with doctor's excuse or parent's note), or absence from school. No mariachi students can ever play (while enrolled in school) with a professional mariachi due to conflict of interest.

Discipline

Exemplary behavior is expected of all mariachi students at all times. Disciplinary action (or removal from class) will be taken for the following infraction of rules:

1. Disrespectful behavior, such as foul language or abusive gestures toward others.
2. Persistent tardiness/unexcused absences.
3. Misuse of school property/musical instruments.
4. Use of alcohol or drugs.
5. Infraction of district or school rules.
6. Fighting.
7. Horseplaying.
8. Playing someone else's instrument.
9. Receiving a write-up for any discipline problems by another teacher.
10. Eating, drinking, or chewing gum in class (water is an exception).
11. Putting on makeup or getting out a mirror in the room. It will be thrown away.

Grading Policy (See Syllabus)

75 percent—daily participation to include:

- Bringing instrument to school
- Playing instrument in class—in sections, private lessons, individually
- Playing scales, rhythmic patterns, or exercises from appropriate books
- Playing ability and effort displayed in class on instrument (home practice)
- Bringing materials—pencils, books, folders, scale sheets, music, theory books, etc.
- Music theory
- Attitude/Behavior/Performances and rehearsals

25 percent—nine-weeks test and weekly tests to include:

- Music theory
- Playing your instrument

Instruments, Uniforms, Music, and Fees

Students don't have to furnish their own instruments for mariachi but are encouraged to do so if they can afford it. Another option is to get a rent-to-own program from a local music store. If students decide to use a school instrument, parents will have to sign a contract holding them responsible for any damages or stolen instruments, and a yearly $25 rental fee will have to be paid in full by the end of October.

- Total Fees = $25 (instrument rental) + $10 (mariachi shirt fee) = $35
- Uniforms will have to be dry-cleaned when turned in (no exceptions).
- Any damages to uniforms or instruments will have to be paid in full by parents or guardians. Any lost music will have to be paid for. All students are required to have music.

Students with "*trajes*":

- *Sombrero* (hat)
- *Moño* (tie)
- *Pantalones, falda* (pants, skirt)
- *Chaleco* (coat)

Students without "*trajes*": black pants + mariachi shirt
All students provide:

- Long-sleeved white shirt with a collar
- Belt and black boots (*botines*)

If you have any questions, please call the school or set up an appointment.

MARIACHI INTEREST INVENTORY

Name_____ Date_____ Instrument_____Period__

The following questions are designed to help me get to know you better.

1. What do you like most about mariachi?
2. What do you dislike most about mariachi?
3. Who is your favorite mariachi?
4. Who is your favorite mariachi singer?
5. What is your favorite mariachi song?
6. Have you ever seen a live mariachi perform in a concert? Who?
7. Can you name three important mariachis?
8. What do you want to accomplish this year?
9. What do you need to do to accomplish that goal?
10. How do you feel about practicing at home?
11. How many minutes or hours do you usually practice at home?
12. Do you have to be told to practice, or do you do it on your own?
13. Did you practice your instrument this summer?
14. Do you practice singing at home?
15. Does anyone in your family play in a mariachi? Who?
16. Do you like to sing? Do you know Spanish?
17. How many mariachi songs can you name that you have played before?
18. How many of these songs have you memorized?
19. Do you own a mariachi CD? Which one(s)?
20. What type of music do you like to hear at home?

LITERACY TEST

Name_____Date_____

Draw the following clefs:

Treble Clef   Bass Clef   Alto Clef   Percussion Clef

What is another name for bass clef?

What is another name for treble clef?

_____

Name one instrument that plays in treble clef.

_____

Five lines and four spaces are called

_____.

Plural of *staff* is

_____.

You count lines and spaces from

_____.

Middle line in treble clef is letter _____.

The musical alphabet has _____ letters. What are they?

When you get to G, where do you go? _____ to

_____

Clefs are placed at the _____ of the staff.

Two staves connected with a brace are called the

_____.

Lines above or below the staff to extend the staff are called

_____.

3

Choosing Appropriate Repertoire

Mark Fogelquist

Recently, a friend commented on the success of a student ensemble at a local mariachi festival. He had seen the group take first place and receive standing ovations at several events. "They don't play fair," he said. "They know which songs to pick." This nonmusician aficionado (a cement contractor) made an important point. Choosing appropriate repertoire is as important for a mariachi educator as it is for the director of a professional mariachi.

Teaching is made infinitely easier if music is well selected. A mariachi educator must look for music that has impact, matches the technical level of his or her players and singers, and allows the educator to teach the fundamentals of mariachi style and build technique. Well-chosen music motivates students to practice and increases the likelihood of successful performances. Songs that are deeply felt by the performers and connect with audiences can reap enormous dividends.

GUIDELINES FOR CHOOSING REPERTOIRE

1. Begin with Observation

The better you know the mariachi repertoire, the better you will be able to choose the right songs for your students. Mariachi conferences and festivals around the United States offer performances by world-class mariachis and outstanding student groups. (For a schedule of conferences, see www.mariachi.org or www.menc.org/mariachi.) Similarly, recordings of great mariachis, new and old, are readily available, making the vast repertoire of Mexico's "national music" accessible even to people living in areas far from Mexico.

2. Start with Mariachi "Standards"

Your group, once it learns a handful of songs, will be asked to perform at a variety of events. Whether at a small family gathering or at a large civic function, your group will be expected to know certain songs. Teaching time-tested "standards" will also serve your students after they leave your school program. Avoid devoting precious rehearsal time to mounting songs that are part of a passing rage or offbeat numbers that have been discarded by the mariachi public, except for the occasional "gem" that has been passed over and deserves revival.

3. Use Standard Arrangements

Most "standards" have been recorded by numerous artists. Seek out and use the one recording that has become the model for the majority of practicing mariachis. The following artists are good models for the mariachi genres noted:

- *Rancheras*: José Alfredo Jiménez has contributed the largest number of songs to the standard repertoire and has recorded the best versions of those songs.
- *Sones, huapangos, joropos,* and *potpourrís*: Mariachi Vargas de Tecalitlán has served as the model for these styles.
- Polkas and *pasodobles*: Mariachi México

- *Boleros*: Javier Solís
- Newer *rancheras*: Vicente Fernández
- Overall: Pedro Infante, Jorge Negrete, Amalia Mendoza, Miguel Aceves Mejía, and Linda Ronstadt's influential album, *Canciones de mi Padre*

Many mariachi standards, since derived from rural folk music, are technically simple and need little or no reworking to fall within the technical grasp of modestly accomplished students. Others can be modified by placing melodies down an octave, inverting parts, changing keys, or eliminating occasional virtuosic elements without losing the essence of the song.

4. Balance Your Repertoire

Students should learn many genres, and your performances will benefit from variety. The main mariachi genres are described below.

Son Jalisciense *(sohn hah-lee-SYEN-seh)*

The *son jalisciense*, which is the *son* form from Jalisco state, is the quintessential mariachi genre. No group is truly a mariachi until it has mastered the *son*. Marked by the driving alternation between 3/4 and 6/8 rhythms, the *son* is the ultimate mariachi expression of *alegría*, or joy. *Sones* include numerous stylistic elements: fast tempos; sharply tongued articulation in the trumpets; aggressive bowing in the violins; exuberant singing; and complicated syncopations and counterrhythms for the guitar, *vihuela*, and *guitarrón*.

Canción Ranchera *(or simply* Ranchera*) (cahn-SYON rahn-CHEH-ra)*

The *canción ranchera* is the emotionally charged personal outpouring of the singer and is the most commonly heard genre of mariachi music. The *ranchera* may be very simple, often using only two chords, and is usually the entry-level song type for beginning mariachi students. In spite of their simplicity, the impact of well-chosen *rancheras* can be amazingly strong and depends primarily on the feeling projected by the singer(s). Three types of *armonía* accompaniment are found: the 3/4 *ranchera valseada* (waltz rhythm), the 2/4 *ranchera polqueada* (polka rhythm), and the slow 4/4 *ranchera*.

"Ella," "El Rey," "Tú Sólo Tú," "Los Laureles," "El Herradero," "Por un Amor," "Volver, Volver," "Camino de Guanajuato," "Caminos de Michoacán," and "Paloma Negra" are frequently requested examples that belong in every group's repertoire.

Bolero *(boh-LEH-roh)*

The mariachi *bolero* is a romantic song in 4/4 time. Rhythmically, the *bolero* is simple to execute, yet the chordal vocabulary is much richer than in the *ranchera* and may present difficulties for beginning students. As with the *ranchera*, impact depends on the ability of the singer to project the meaning of the lyrics. "Sabor a Mí," "Gema," "Cerca Del Mar," "Sin Ti," "Solamente Una Vez," "De Qué Manera te Olvido," "Por Mujeres Como Tú," "Reloj," and "Si Nos Dejan" are frequently requested standards.

Corrido *(coh-RIH-doh)*

The mariachi *corrido* is musically similar to the *ranchera*. The distinguishing characteristic between the genres lies in the lyrics. The *corrido* is a narrative song type, and its verses relate a series of events. *Corridos* deal with historical events, such as the Mexican Revolution, or with personal experiences of significance. A whole body of *corridos* is devoted to famous horses, while more recently, drug or people smuggling or the events related to 9/11 have been favorite topics. Not all *corridos* are appropriate for students. Some well-known *corridos* appropriate for student groups are "Siete Leguas," "Carabina Treinta Treinta," and "El Caballo Blanco."

Polka

The polka is very effectively rendered by the mariachi, and several examples should be part of every group's repertoire. As an instrumental genre with an upbeat tempo, polkas encourage animated audience participation and even dancing. They also allow singers a chance to rest—

an important consideration for student mariachis that may rely heavily on one or two solo singers. The polka may require fairly advanced technique from the violins and especially the trumpets, but some examples, such as "Jesusita en Chihuahua," "Las Perlitas," and "El Garabato," can be successfully played by intermediate mariachi students.

Vals *(VAHLS)*

Like the polka, the Mexican waltz (*vals*) is effectively rendered by the mariachi. Even a beginning mariachi should be able to play at least one waltz since student groups are frequently asked to entertain at *quinceañeras*, the elaborate celebration of a girl's fifteenth birthday, which in Mexican culture symbolizes her transition from girlhood to womanhood. "Alejandra," "Sentimiento," "Dios Nunca Muere," and "Viva mi Desgracia" are good examples of Mexican waltzes. "Aniversario," while not of Mexican origin, should be included in a group's repertoire if it is going to play at family celebrations.

Huapango *(wah-PAHN-goh)*

The *huapango* is the mariachi adaptation of the *son huasteco* and a first cousin of the *son jalisciense*. The accompaniment by the rhythm section features alternating 3/4 and 6/8 rhythms, and syncopation is common. The element that distinguishes the *huapango* from the *son jalisciense* is the use of the *apagón* (ah-pa-GOHN), or damping of guitar and *vihuela* strings immediately after certain chords are sounded. The *apagón* softens the aggressive drive characteristic of the *son jalisciense* and creates subtle rhythmic shifts. *Huapangos* also feature virtuosic violin melodies and falsetto singing. This genre is generally appropriate for advanced groups. The two most requested *huapangos* in the mariachi repertoire are "La Malagueña" and "Cucurrucucú Paloma."

Joropo *(hoh-ROH-poh)*

The *joropo* is of Venezuelan origin and entered the mariachi repertoire in the early 1970s at a time when the Mariachi Vargas de Tecalitlán made extended annual tours to Venezuela. The *joropo* is similar to the *huapango* in many ways, including the use of *apagón*, shifting 3/4 and 6/8 rhythms, syncopation, and counterrhythms. Many mariachi *joropos* use complicated harmonies and unusual melodies derived from jazz and international pop music, as this genre entered the mariachi repertoire when a good deal of experimentation was taking place. This genre is for advanced student ensembles. The most commonly played *joropos* are "La Bikina," "La Fuente," "La Gruta," "Alma Llanera," and "Mi Ciudad."

Pasodoble *(pah-soh-DOH-bleh)*

The *pasodoble* is an instrumental genre of Spanish origin and is rhythmically similar to the polka. In a classic *pasodoble*, an opening section in the minor mode features a brilliant trumpet melody, while the second section in the relative major begins with the violins. The *pasodoble* can be of great impact when well played but is usually reserved for advanced students.

"El Dos Negro" and "España Cañí" are *pasodobles* that I have seen effectively performed by student mariachis. "El Niño Perdido" is one of the most requested pieces in the entire mariachi repertoire, though not strictly a *pasodoble*. "El Zopilote Mojado," another frequently requested piece, is a cross between a *pasodoble* and polka. Both pieces require advanced trumpet players but are not out of reach for some student mariachis.

Danzón *(dahn-SOHN)*

The *danzón* is a dance genre of Cuban origin based on an asymmetrical division of the 4/4 measure: 3 + 3 + 2 (eighth notes). Although much more popular a generation ago, I have seen the *danzón* used successfully as a show piece by one or two student mariachis. The unusual rhythms, brilliant trumpet parts, and high-register violin melodies are only for advanced-level players. The two best-known *danzones* are "Juárez" and "Nereidas."

Cumbia *(COOM-byah)*

The *cumbia* entered the mariachi repertoire in the middle 1970s with the smash hit, "El Mariachi Loco" (yes, "El Mariachi Loco" is over thirty years old). Based on a Colombian dance genre, it achieved early success, faded, and has been revived by student mariachis in the United States during the last decade. While appropriate for backyard parties or dances, my personal feeling is that it does not belong in concerts, an opinion supported by the Albuquerque Mariachi Conference, where it is banned from the student mariachi competition. In addition to "El Mariachi Loco," a number of *cumbias* have been recorded by the Mariachi Vargas, Mariachi México, and Mariachi Nuevo Tecalitlán.

Son Jarocho *(sohn hah-ROH-choh)*

The *son jarocho* is the regional variant of the Mexican *son* found in Veracruz. It has been effectively adapted for the mariachi, with the intricate harp and *requinto* melodies of the *conjunto jarocho* being given to the mariachi violins and less often the trumpets. The *jarocho* concept of solo improvisation by individual instruments allows each section of the mariachi to demonstrate its technical skill. The best-known *son jarocho* in the mariachi repertoire is "El Cascabel," which features a succession of virtuoso solos by each of the mariachi instruments. This piece is often attempted by students who do not have sufficient technique, and the results are frequently unsatisfactory to say the least. Directors wishing to mount "El Cascabel" should eliminate one or more of the solos if students are not capable of executing them with aplomb.

Potpourrí *(*Popurrí*) (poh-purr-EE)*

With the proliferation of mariachi festivals during the past twenty-five years, top-level professional mariachis have been pitted against one another in large venues ever more frequently. To maximize limited time slots, these groups frequently create medleys (*potpourrís*) from segments of well-known songs. These arrangements have become ever more elaborate and virtuosic, both instrumentally and vocally.

The *potpourrí*, in most cases, should only be attempted by advanced-level students. Early *potpourrís* from the Mariachi Vargas album *Fiesta en Jalisco* include "Allá en el Rancho," "Cielito Lindo," "Los Buenos Vecinos," and "Mis Caballos." Subsequent recordings by the Mariachi Vargas include "Viva Veracruz," "Que Viva Veracruz II," and "Veracruz III." Almost all major mariachis have recorded *potpourrís*.

5. Evaluate Your Selections

Ask yourself these questions:

- Will all or most of your students be able to play or sing all of the notes?
- Will all or most of your students be able to play and sing all of the notes in tune?
- Will all or most of your students be able to stay together rhythmically?

If your answer to any of these questions is "no," you should rethink your repertoire choices. I will never forget the comments of Jesús Rodríguez de Híjar, one of the greatest mariachi arrangers in history, when asked to evaluate groups at the Tucson Mariachi Conference. After hearing a university mariachi attempt to play "Violín Huapango," a very complicated number, he said: "You must learn to crawl before you try to run." While it is good to challenge students, repertoire choices should not be so far from the mark that they teach students to "fake it." Bad performances teach bad habits—everything in due time.

WHERE TO OBTAIN MUSIC

A good deal of music, especially for mariachi standards, is available through the Mariachi Publishing Company (www.mariachimusica.com) and the Mariachi Connection (www.mariachiconnection.com). Unfortunately, few of the transcriptions or arrangements offered here have been subjected to the editorial process that controls major publications of band, choral, or orchestra music. Errors are common, and many of the arrangements—for copyright reasons—are nonstandard. For additional resources, see the Sheet Music and Methods page on the MENC Mariachi Web site.

The single best source of mariachi scores and parts is mariachi conferences. At most conferences where workshops are offered, enrolled students are given a workbook of transcriptions for their instruments. Scores and full sets of parts are usually available to mariachi educators for a fee. This money is extremely well spent since scores offered at mariachi conferences are transcriptions made by active professionals of stature, are used by well-known groups, or are transcriptions of famous recordings.

The next best source of music is the archives of veteran mariachi educators, such as the contributors to this book; you can contact them at the mariachi forum on the MENC Mariachi Web site. For beginning mariachi educators, nothing is more important than connecting with individuals who have already worked in the field for a number of years, both in terms of getting materials and in getting advice.

4

Preparing for a Performance

Sergio "Checo" Alonso

You've spent countless hours rehearsing your students, and now they're ready to play for the public. How do you prepare them for the performance?

As a mariachi educator, you have the special responsibility of preparing your students to perform at the many cultural, celebratory, and religious events in their communities. Some are formal and occur onstage, while others celebrate life events in private homes. Because mariachis play such an important role in these events, your students need special attention to properly prepare for the different situations in which they may be asked to perform.

A successful performance is the result of strong guidance and hard work. Your students will reap the rewards of increased confidence and motivation as you prepare them for the demands of mariachi performance.

REHEARSAL STRATEGIES

1. Set Realistic Expectations

No one knows the skill levels of your students better than you do. Avoid "biting off more than you can chew" by not overloading students with new music or music that is beyond their technical reach. Plenty of standard mariachi works meet the needs of every student, from beginner to advanced. Make your decisions based on the ability levels of most of your students, and plan your song selection accordingly.

2. Prepare the Music

After finding skill-level-appropriate music, if you feel that some aspects are not suitable, feel free to make necessary changes to meet the needs of your ensemble. Transposing to a different key for a singer, inverting a trumpet part, bringing a violin melody down an octave, and simplifying harmony in the rhythm section are but a few ways you can modify the music without watering it down. Having a strong grasp of the stylistic elements for each genre will guarantee that any changes you make won't affect the integrity of the piece.

3. Manage Your Time

Preparing for a *chamba* (gig) entails developing repertoire for a set amount of performance time. Spend less time working on warm-ups, fundamentals, and exercises and more time working on actual songs. Be conscious of how long it usually takes your students to read through a piece and how long they need to memorize their music and lyrics. You will then have a good idea of how much rehearsal time will be needed to learn and polish the required number of songs.

4. Set Priorities: Quality versus Quantity

Ideally, you want to build a polished, carefully selected, and tightly executed collection of songs. You may, however, be forced to choose between cohesiveness and repertoire development when placed under time constraints. Judge what's more important for your particular event—spending time polishing a few songs or mounting numerous new songs. Just be careful not to sacrifice too much of either.

5. Conduct Sectionals

Depending on the song, some sections will learn their parts with ease, whereas others will struggle. Allocate additional time and attention to those instrumentalists who need it the most by holding sectionals. The violins (the largest section) will usually require more focused rehearsal time to address the demands of their often complex arrangements.

6. Practice in Performance Formation

Before your performance, arrange your students in the standing formation while running through your music. Typically, you will position them in a single concert arc, but if you have limited space, two arcs are also common. Your students will benefit from listening to and watching each other in the same manner that they will during an actual performance, not to mention that they will look very professional when they know exactly where and how to stand.

ATTIRE

The contemporary mariachi attire is adopted from that of the *charro* (Mexican cowboy) and consists of *chaleco* (jacket) and *pantalones* (pants) for the men and a long *falda* (skirt) for the women. While some accessories are optional, no *traje de charro* (*charro* suit) is complete without *botines* (boots), *moño* (bow), in some cases *botonadura* (metallic button adornments), and *cinto piteado* (belt) for the men. A fully accessorized *charro* suit, complete with vest and *sombrero* (hat), can get into the hundreds, even thousands of dollars. Budget permitting, you should showcase your group in the full traditional attire. However, if resources are limited, you do have options.

The following is a list of what to wear:

1. For the modest budget, have your students wear a simple white dress shirt, black pants or skirt, and black shoes. Complement the attire with a colored *moño*, which costs anywhere from $5–15.

2. Complement black pants or skirt and black shoes with a *pachuqueña*, a traditional button-down shirt worn by the *caporal* (ranch foreman). Prices range from $15–30.
3. Upgrade to the full *traje de caporal* (*caporal* suit) by complementing the *pachuqueña* with the traditional pants, boots ($30–$60), and *cinto piteado* (starting at about $50). A complete *caporal* suit ranges from $200–300.
4. The *traje de gala* style *charro* suit is the most widely used and is characterized by the silver or gold adornments worn along the seams of the pants, as the jacket buckles, and, in most cases, on the sleeves. While black is the most universal, you can find it in almost any color. A three-piece suit begins at about $250.
5. The most elegant (and expensive) suits are the *traje de greca* (leather or ultrasuede appliqué) and *traje bordado con hilo metálico* (embroidered with metallic thread), which are embellished with intricately embroidered designs. A matching *sombrero* ($100–200) will add a touch of refinement to this suit. These suits begin at about $400.

Two excellent sources for high-quality mariachi suits are Mariachi Connection (www.mariachiconnection.com) and La Casa del Mariachi (www.casadelmariachi.com).

ETIQUETTE

The performance begins the minute your students arrive at the event, so ensure they make a good first impression by talking to them beforehand about proper etiquette. Students must arrive with clean suits and *moños* and polished boots, and they must make sure that their *botonadura* is in good condition. Ladies generally wear their hair pulled back, showing off matching earrings. The gentlemen should be clean shaven and, if necessary, with hair pulled back as well. Above all else, students should understand that they are representatives of their school and should behave in a professional manner. Whether it is arriving on time to the event or dealing with excessively demanding clients, your students should always carry themselves with integrity, self-respect, and class.

IDENTIFY THE PERFORMANCE

A key step in preparing for a successful performance is to identify the type of event. Mariachi ensembles are often asked to play in significantly different scenarios, and each may influence your selection of songs and your approach to preparing your students.

The most common type of event is the celebration, such as wedding receptions and *quinceañeras*. For this type of festive occasion, make sure to discuss the concert expectations of the organizer. You may be asked to perform ambiance music during the cocktail hour, familiar crowd pleasers during dinner, or perhaps more upbeat music at a dance. Ascertaining the needs of the organizer will help you determine whether you need to prepare soft instrumentals as opposed to a set of *ranchera* and *bolero* favorites or even danceable *sones*, *cumbias*, and polkas. You might even ask if the majority of the audience is from a certain region, so you can be sure to play a song from that region.

In addition to typical celebrations, you may be asked to perform at a mass, a *serenata* (serenade), a funeral, or perhaps onstage in a concert setting. Whatever the occasion, choosing and preparing the right repertoire will enhance your performance and the experience of your audience.

PREPARING FOR A STAGE PERFORMANCE

Performing onstage is a special opportunity to show off the artistry and skill of your mariachi, whether they play at a community festival, a performing arts center, or in a school assembly. Because your group is the show, they must attract and hold the attention of their audience, and doing so requires additional preparation.

Stage performances offer you the opportunity to select your songs and showcase the results of your students' hard work. The performance will probably consist of standard crowd pleasers, but it can also include more complex "show songs." Because these show songs require a higher level of technical skill, they should be performed by the most advanced students.

Some of the most popular ones include "Viva Veracruz," "Que Viva Veracruz II," "Veracruz III," "Cielito Lindo Huasteco," "Fiesta en Jalisco," "Violin Huapango," "El Cascabel," "Bodas de Luis Alonso," and "Huapango de Moncayo."
The following are suggestions for a successful stage performance.

1. Balance Your Set

Go through your ready stock of songs, and put together a set list that combines different genres and/or incorporates a variety of new pieces. Consider carefully the flow of your set as you move from one song to another. Mix upbeat genres (*sones*, *rancheras polqueadas*, *joropos*, polkas, or medleys) with slower, more lyrical ones (*boleros*, *huapangos*, and *rancheras*).

2. Highlight Your Strengths

Your time is limited, so showcase your best performers. A *pasodoble* or polka will highlight a strong trumpet section, while a fine violin section may shine during a *son jarocho* or *huapango*. Select your best vocalists to sing both solos and in chorus to showcase the group's vocal strength.

3. Polish, Polish, Polish

A set repertoire will enable you to dedicate more time to perfecting your performance. Because this is a heightened level of performance, pay special attention to all of the finer points in music making, including articulation, dynamics, phrasing, expression, blend, and balance.

4. Stress Stage Presence

Charisma onstage makes a big statement. Encourage your students to carry themselves with poise by smiling and physically expressing what they sing. Performers should stand tall, with feet shoulder-width apart and with everyone in the section holding their instrument uniformly and acknowledging the audience. Discourage negative gestures such as slouching, grimacing after a missed note, or turning your back to the audience. Most important, performers must have fun! An energetic group that exudes confidence will captivate the audience.

5. Provide a Stage Plot

Where microphones are available, provide stage crews and sound engineers with a stage plot. The typical show setup is a single arc with three vocal microphones in the middle of the stage in front of the ensemble. Every instrumentalist is amplified, and there are optional vocal microphones for the rhythm section. For proper microphone positioning, stands with boom arms should be used for the violin and rhythm sections. Setup may vary depending on the size and instrumentation of your group, microphone availability, and individual needs.

6. Run a Sound Check

High-quality sound mixes and amplification are an important part of presenting a great stage performance. Whenever possible, run a sound check to test the audio system. Start by having members of your group play into each microphone individually, and then move on to play as sections. Establish a blend within each section, and close the sound check by having the full ensemble play. Express your needs to the sound engineer throughout the process, especially when balancing the levels of the monitors and side fills. Spending focused time on the sound check will better prepare your group and the sound crew for the performance.

7. Practice Stage Maneuvering and Microphone Manipulation

Nothing looks more professional than a group that knows how to confidently move around onstage and properly handle microphones. Equipment, such as monitors, cables, and microphone stands, sometimes hinders mobility, so investing time in walking through your set will help minimize any insecurity during the performance.

These are suggestions for maneuvering onstage and using microphones:

- Position solo, duet, and trio singing on the front vocal microphones.
- Violin and trumpet microphones may double as voice mics for chorus parts.
- Use front vocal mics for instrumental solos.
- Be aware of the location of monitors, cables, and stands.
- Take adequate time when walking to a vocal mic.

PREPARING FOR A PRIVATE ENGAGEMENT

There are many different types of private events if your school allows you to perform at these. In many cases, your hosts choose the songs, and the only way to prepare is to rehearse what you think you may be asked to play based on the nature of the event. Other seasonal events, however, require you to adhere to a particular set of songs. For example, *Fiestas Patrias* (patriotic holidays) and *Día de Las Madres* (Mother's Day) require music that fits the general theme of the holiday, while others, like *Día de La Virgen de Guadalupe* (the Feast of the Virgin of Guadalupe) and *Las Posadas* (a Christmas tradition) require a strict set of religious songs.

The following are suggested songs for your performance.

1. The Festive Gathering

Whether performing for a wedding or a birthday party, expect to play the standards. The demographics of your audience and the general mood of the event will influence what songs are requested. In general, you can count on playing such pieces as "Camino de Guanajuato," "Cucurrucucú Paloma," "El Rey," "Ella," "Guadalajara," "La Malagueña," "El Mariachi Loco," and "Volver, Volver."

2. The Mass

The traditional "mariachi mass," or *Misa Panamericana*, is commonly performed at baptisms, weddings, and *quinceañeras* within the Roman

Catholic Church. Unlike other performances, at a mass you will accompany the religious service with specific sacred music, such as "Angelus," "Señor, Ten Piedad," "Gloria," "Aleluya," "Padre Nuestro," "Santo," "Cordero de Dios," "Ave María," and "Pescador de Hombres."

3. The Serenata

Countless love songs in the mariachi repertoire can be used at the *serenata* (serenade). While historically a courtship occasion, your early morning performance may also entail playing "Las Mañanitas" (Mexican birthday song) to celebrate the dawn of a new birthday. Some classic love songs include "Despierta," "Serenata Sin Luna," "Serenata Huasteca," "Gema," "Solamente Una Vez," "Reloj," "Sin Ti," "Tres Regalos," and "La Gloria Eres Tú."

4. The Funeral

Perhaps the most emotional performance is a funeral at which friends and family say farewell with music that had special meaning to the departed. Songs that mourn the loss but also celebrate the life of a loved one include "Amor Eterno," "Un Día a la Vez," "Despedida con Mariachi," "Te Vas Angel Mío," "Cruz de Madera," "Nadie Es Eterno," "Adiós a la Vida," "La Barca de Oro," and "Las Golondrinas."

TAKE IT FROM THE PROFESSIONALS

The best way for your students to learn the "dos" and "don'ts" of a successful performance is by observing professional groups.

On Video

Mariachi Jalisciense (www.jalisciense.com) has a superb collection of free online video-clip performances from some of the most renowned mariachi ensembles. Mariachi Publishing (www.mariachieducationresources.com) also has some educational videos that include performances.

En Vivo (Live Performance)

Nothing beats watching and listening to a live performance. Sit in with a local mariachi group, or observe one in a public performance at a restaurant or community festival. Mariachi conferences are also a great source of superb performances of mariachi groups of all different age and skill levels. The more your students are exposed to the world of mariachi, the more they will learn about how and what to prepare for their own performances.

5

Teaching the Beginning *Guitarrón*

John A. Vela

The *guitarrón* (ghee-tah-ROHN) is a large, six-string Mexican bass guitar characterized by a vaulted back and short, fretless fingerboard. It was most likely developed in the southwestern region of Mexico during the latter half of the nineteenth century and was largely responsible for supplanting the more unwieldy harp as the bass-note provider in the mariachi ensemble. Early *guitarrones* had five gut strings, the lower three metal-wound, and the sound board was left unvarnished. Its traditional construction was probably modeled after that of the small, five-string Mexican guitar called the *vihuela* (vee-WEH-lah), which is, in turn, descended from the archaic Spanish *vihuela de mano*.

The performance technique of the early *guitarrón* consisted of plucking single strings to produce notes. As the instrument evolved into the twentieth century, however, a sixth string was added, and the associated performance technique was adapted accordingly. This is known as the "double-string" technique and features pairs of strings plucked in octaves. The modern-day *guitarrón* has six strings, three of which are nylon wound. The other three are metal wound and are available in copper, brass, bronze, or steel. The purpose of playing strings in pairs is to project greater volume since bass notes are typically difficult to hear, especially when performed in support of the melodic lines of the trumpets and violins of the mariachi ensemble.

Natividad (Nati) Santiago (1941–1993), former *guitarronista* of the renowned Mariachi Vargas de Tecalitlán, was influential in pioneering and popularizing the double-string technique of *guitarrón* playing. In 1983, Nati published his *Método Práctico de Guitarrón* (*Practical Method for Guitarrón*). From 1959 until 1993, he recorded thousands of songs and has accompanied most of the major Mexican *ranchera* artists. Nati once suggested to me that the characteristic tone of the *guitarrón* might best be expressed by the syllable *tan* (tahn); the *t* sound represents the attack and articulation of the higher-pitched nylon string, while the *an* sound reflects the depth and resonance of the accompanying, lower-pitched metal string.

SELECTING A *GUITARRÓN*

Here are a few things to consider when selecting a *guitarrón*. The better-sounding instruments typically feature a Spanish cedar back and sides, a mahogany neck, a rosewood fingerboard, and a *tacote* top. "Entry-level," or student instruments, imported from Mexico or, more recently, from China are available for purchase and are usually adequate for beginners. The action and setup on these instruments are often acceptable, but the tone and projection are not, of course, comparable to "step-up" or professional models.

When trying out an instrument, pluck each open string. The tone should be clear and steady with a long sustain, about five to seven seconds. Any buzzing or rattling or a muted tone might indicate an inferior instrument or a "bad" string. Be sure to visually inspect the entire instrument inside and out, looking for signs of good craftsmanship and attention to detail. Ensure that the instrument does not have cracks, twisted or warped wood, or indications of repairs or patchwork. Check to see that the strings at the bridge are spaced evenly and the string holes are perfectly aligned.

String spacing at the nut should also be equidistant. Between the neck joint and the sound hole, string height should be set between ½" and ⅝" above the sounding board. Setting the action any higher will adversely affect intonation and unnecessarily test the player's strength and endurance. If the strings are set lower, they may tend to slap against the sounding board during performance. The *guitarrón* may be fitted with either metal tuning machines or wooden pegs.

Most student instruments and some professional models feature metal tuning machines. These are recommended for beginners since they promote better intonation and they are much easier to use than wooden tuning pegs. It is important that the tuning keys turn smoothly, without any kinking, slipping, or binding. Gears on inexpensive tuning machines tend to strip very easily and eventually will need to be replaced. Better-quality tuning machines are identifiable by their price; budget permitting, these are certainly worth the added expense.

Tuning machines are customarily installed in one of the following two ways:

1. "Classic guitar" style (also called an "open tuning head"), in which two channels are cut into the headstock and tuning machines are fitted horizontally or
2. "Retro-fitted" style, in which holes are drilled into the head and the tuning machine posts are inserted vertically (this also may be the result of converting a "peg" *guitarrón* by inserting machine heads into the original peg holes).

Retro-fitted *guitarrones* are sometimes more difficult to string, as the posts are frequently too short to accommodate the heavy-gauge strings. Furthermore, retro-fitted tuning keys protrude laterally, not front to back, which may ultimately render the headstock too wide to fit in its case. If the *guitarrón* has wooden pegs, it is important that the pegs be custom-fitted to the peg holes. That is, the pegs should have a taper that matches the taper of the peg holes. Poorly trained luthiers turning out inferior instruments frequently drill cylindrical peg holes and pair them with often hand-carved, tapered wooden pegs that tend to slip and wobble and not hold the correct pitch.

CARING FOR YOUR *GUITARRÓN*

Proper care of the *guitarrón* is essential for several reasons. Although it is large in size, the *guitarrón* is more delicate and susceptible to incidental damage than nearly all the other instruments of the mariachi ensemble. Precisely because of its size and exotic construction characteristics, many conventional luthiers and music store personnel may shy away from attempting repairs on a *guitarrón* simply due to their lack of familiarity with it.

Because the climate of the region in which many *guitarrones* are constructed may differ greatly from that in which you will be holding your classes, cracking or splitting of the *guitarrón's* sides and back is not unusual. This becomes increasingly true as the instrument ages and the wood dries more thoroughly. Considering the fact that many student-level *guitarrones* are made of wood from cool and humid southwestern Mexico (Paracho, Michoacán, comes to mind) and many North American mariachi classes are conducted in hot and dry locales (think: Texas, New Mexico, and Arizona), careful attention to temperature and humidity is essential. Here are some general guidelines:

- Keep the instrument in its case or "gig bag" (and the storage closet) when not in use.
- Keep the instrument away from excessive heat or cold.
- Adjust the humidity of the storage facility (violin humidifiers may be an option).
- Never leave the instrument leaning against a wall (or *anywhere* it might fall over).

- When connecting the strap, always hold the instrument with your hand.
- Acquire and install standard guitar "strap locks" to avoid accidental dropping.
- Change the strings when they begin to sound dull or "dead."
- Maintain a supply of extra metal fourth strings, as these tend to break far more frequently than all others (students should carry spares in their cases to performances, in case of emergencies).
- Treat the instrument as you would a baby; both are very delicate.

SELECTING YOUR *GUITARRÓN* PLAYER

Now that you've got your *guitarrón*, it's time to decide which of your students has what it takes to anchor your mariachi ensemble as your *guitarronista* for years to come. Prerequisite qualities to look for in prospective *guitarrón* students might include the following:

- Persistence and determination to "stick with it" since it takes time to develop the calluses on the fingertips and thumbs necessary to perform comfortably;
- A good sense of timing and rhythmic coordination, leading to the ability to feel and consistently produce a strong, steady pulse;
- Good pitch recognition in order to produce octaves—in tune— despite the lack of a fretted fingerboard; and
- Strong sense of reliability and responsibility to the group, with exemplary records with respect to school attendance, citizenship, and academics. (Your *guitarrón* player is probably the *one* performer you can least afford to lose for academic or disciplinary reasons.)

Teachers might do well to attempt to identify double-jointed students, as they are likely to experience difficulty fingering certain notes. Left-handed students will need to have their instruments restrung in the opposite direction and taught in a "mirrored" fashion, where carrying position and fingerings are reversed. Neither physical size nor gender should present problems, however, as the *guitarrón* is not as heavy as it looks. The teacher need only remind doubtful students that the part of the instrument that makes it look so big and intimidating is the resonating cavity—and that consists primarily of air.

GUITARRÓN PERFORMANCE POSTURE

Now it's time to actually pick up the *guitarrón*, strap it on, and learn to play—it's much easier to teach it once you can play it yourself! Proper performance posture for the *guitarrón* includes the following:

- Both feet flat on floor, shoulder-width apart;
- Knees slightly bent, never locked;
- Back straight and tall;
- Hips pushed slightly forward;
- Shoulders back and relaxed; and
- Chin up and eyes forward.

There are two ways of supporting the *guitarrón* with a strap. One is to simply place the strap over the right shoulder, and the other is to place the strap over both the left shoulder and across the back. I once asked Nati why he favored the former method, and he replied, "it's easier to place the strap over the right shoulder quickly without having to take off your *sombrero*." On the other hand, I prefer the "over the left shoulder and across the back" method. It's not only more comfortable for me, but when I tried the other way, I felt that I had to "hunch" my right shoulder to keep the strap from slipping off. That created a lot of tension in my neck, shoulder, and back.

The *guitarrón* should rest on the right side of the abdomen between the ribcage and navel, while the nut is aligned with the left shoulder. The strap runs parallel along the side of the instrument. The sound hole should be facing upward at approximately a 45° angle.

From the player's perspective, the right hand is turned slightly to the left, the forearm resting lightly on the edge of the *guitarrón* on the right side of the downward curve of the middle bout, or waist. The right hand is arched over the sound hole, with the thumb extended to the left. The *guitarronero*'s right thumb should *always be extended*! Generally speaking, the fingers are positioned above and perpendicular to the strings, while the thumb is parallel to and beside them. The left hand cradles the neck in a *U* shape, with the thumb and index finger aligned with the nut. The left wrist is bent slightly upward, the left palm facing the neck. The left elbow hangs loosely alongside the ribcage.

TUNING THE *GUITARRÓN*

The *guitarrón* may be tuned with a piano or electronic tuner. Some electronic tuners have a mic input that can be connected to a transducer mic. These mics are fairly inexpensive and will allow the instrument to be tuned without any interference from outside noise.

GUITARRÓN NOTATION

Guitarrón music is notated in the bass clef. Normally, the lower note of each octave is written, but it is general practice to play *both* strings. The exception to the rule is single-fingered notes, such as G♯. There are also instances when an arranger might call for a single-string effect, which would be indicated by the words *single string* or *una cuerda*.

TEACHING THE *GUITARRÓN* FINGERINGS

The following are instructions on teaching the twelve different note fingerings for *guitarrón*. Also included in this chapter is a fingering chart, which may be reproduced, enlarged, and posted for convenient classroom reference.

The first two notes to be learned on the *guitarrón* are the As. The high A is played with the first (A) string open, and the low A is played with the sixth (A) string open as well. The right-hand middle finger will pluck the first string with the tip of the finger, and the right thumb will contact the sixth string at a 45° angle. It may be stated as a general rule, that:

- The right-hand middle finger plucks *only* the first string;
- The second and third strings will *always* be plucked with the right index finger; and
- The fourth, fifth, and sixth strings are *always* plucked with the right thumb.

The thumb must be extended outward, allowing the flat part ("thumb pad") of the tip joint to contact the string. Pull the strings toward each other in a diagonal, upward motion, bending the right wrist slightly upward and releasing the strings simultaneously. Make sure both strings are played with equal volume. Also make sure that the left-hand thumb and fingers do not touch the vibrating A strings. Allow the strings to vibrate for four full counts and relax the right hand on the release.

The next two notes to be learned are the Ds. The high D is fingered with the pad of the left-hand middle, or second, finger on the third (C) string about 2¼" from the nut, and the low D is played with the fifth (D) string open. Simulated "fret" markers, made of colored vinyl or masking tape, can be wrapped around the fingerboard to aid in correct finger placement, just as violin teachers do for their beginning students. The right index finger will pluck the third string, and the thumb will contact the fifth string at a 45° angle. The thumb must be extended outward, allowing the thumb pad to contact the string.

Pull the strings toward each other in a diagonal, upward motion, bending the right wrist slightly upward and releasing the strings simultaneously. Make sure both strings are played with equal volume. Allow the strings to vibrate for four full counts, and relax the right hand on the release. Make sure to press the left-hand middle finger firmly.

Next, alternate between A and D. The left middle, or second, finger should hover over the D note on the third string while playing the A notes. Make sure that the left thumb and fingers do not touch the vibrating strings when playing the A notes.

The third pair of notes will be the Gs. The high G is fingered with the pad of the left little, or fourth, finger on the second (E) string, about 4" from the nut, while the low G is played with the fourth (G) string open. The left ring, or third, finger can be placed beside or on top of the little finger to help depress the string. The right index finger will pluck the second string, and the thumb will contact the fourth string at a 45° angle.

The thumb must be extended outward, allowing the thumb pad to contact the string. Pull the strings toward each other in a diagonal, upward motion, bending the right wrist slightly upward and releasing the strings simultaneously. Make sure that both strings are played with equal volume. Again, repeat in whole notes, allowing the strings to vibrate for four full counts and relaxing the right hand on the release. The left-hand ring and little fingers should press the second string firmly.

The next exercise is to alternate between A, D, and G. Repeat this exercise several times. The left middle finger should hover over the D note on the third string, while the left little finger hovers over the G note on second string when playing the A. Make sure that the left thumb and fingers do not touch the vibrating strings when playing the A notes.

The fourth pair of notes will be the Es. The high E is played with the second (E) string open, and the low E is fingered on the fifth (D) string with the left-hand middle and ring fingers. The middle finger will depress the string about 2" from the nut. The ring finger should be placed beside it to add strength and support, the two fingertips depressing the fifth string together. The right index finger will pluck the second string, and the thumb will contact the fifth string at a 45° angle. The thumb must be extended outward, allowing the thumb pad to contact the string. Pull the strings toward each other in a diagonal, upward motion, bending the right wrist slightly upward and releasing the strings simultaneously. Make sure that both strings are played with equal volume. Again, play in whole notes, allowing the strings to vibrate for four full counts and relaxing the right hand on the release.

The next exercise will be to alternate between A, D, G, and E. Play a whole note A, followed by whole notes D, G, and E. Repeat this exercise several times. The left-hand middle finger should hover over the D note on the third string, while the little finger hovers over the G note on the second string when playing an A. Again, make sure that the left thumb and fingers do not interfere with the vibrating A strings. The left hand should not shift and will remain in this "home" position throughout the exercise.

The fifth pair of notes will be the Cs. The high C is played with the third (C) string open, and the low C is fingered with the left thumb pad on the sixth (A) string about 3½" from the nut. The palm of the left hand must press firmly against the neck in a diagonal to provide leverage for the thumb. The right index finger will pluck the third string, and the thumb will contact the sixth string at a 45° angle. The thumb must be extended outward, allowing the thumb pad to contact the string. Pull the strings toward each other in a diagonal, upward motion, bending the right wrist slightly upward and releasing the strings simultaneously. Make sure that both strings are played with equal volume. Again, play in whole notes, pressing the left thumb down firmly, thus allowing the strings to vibrate for four full counts and relaxing the right hand on the release.

The sixth pair of notes will be the Fs. The high F is fingered on the second (E) string with the tip of the left index finger about 1¼" from the nut, and the low F is fingered with the tips of the left middle and ring fingers on the fifth (D) string. The middle finger will depress the fifth string about 3" from the nut, with the ring finger beside it to aid with proper intonation and support. This is the first instance the player does not have the advantage of an open string and, thus, needs to finger both notes. The right index finger will pluck the second string, and the thumb will contact the fifth string at a 45° angle. The thumb must be extended outward, allowing the thumb pad to contact the string. Pull the strings toward each other in a diagonal, upward motion, bending the right wrist slightly upward and releasing the strings simultaneously. Make sure that both strings are played with equal volume. Pay close attention to tone quality and intonation.

The seventh pair of notes will be the Bs. The high B is fingered on the first (A) string with the left-hand middle finger pad about 2½" from the nut. The low B is fingered with the left thumb pad, also 2½" from the nut, on the sixth (A) string. The right middle finger will pluck the first string at the tip joint, and the right thumb will contact the sixth string at a 45° angle. The thumb must be extended outward, allowing the thumb pad to contact the string. Pull the strings toward each other in a diagonal, upward motion, bending the right wrist slightly upward and releasing the strings simultaneously. Make sure that both strings are played with equal volume. Again, allow the strings to vibrate for four full counts, and relax the right hand on the release. Now we can play the C-major scale with all seven notes that we have learned. See figure 5.1 for the scale written in standard *guitarrón* notation.

The eighth pair of notes will be the F♯s (enharmonically G♭). The high F♯ is fingered on the second (E) string with the tip of the left index finger about 2½" from the nut. The low F♯ is fingered with the tips of the left middle and ring fingers on the fifth (D) string about 4" from the nut. The left hand will shift up to this position from the shape formerly learned as F. The right index finger will pluck the second string, and the thumb will contact the fifth string at a 45° angle. Be sure to press the fingers of the left hand down firmly through the duration of each note. The next scale we will play is the G-major scale (see figure 5.2), which has one sharp (F♯).

The ninth pair of notes will be the C♯s (enharmonically D♭). The high C♯ is fingered on the third (C) string with the tip of the left index finger about 1¼" from the nut. The low C♯ is fingered on the sixth (A) string, with the tips of the left middle and ring fingers being forced to stretch about 4" from the nut. Due to the inherent physical difficulty involved in fingering the low C♯ correctly, C♯ is frequently performed on a single string, fingering only the high C♯. The right index finger will pluck the third string, and should the

C Major Scale
Written in standard guitarrón notation

Reminder: Play a pair of strings for each note.

FIGURE 5.1

G Major Scale
Written in standard guitarrón notation

FIGURE 5.2

student become capable of producing the double-note C♯, the right thumb
will contact the sixth string at a 45° angle. As you practice, if you experience
difficulty playing both strings, then play single string. The next scale we
will play is the D-major scale (see figure 5.3), which has two sharps (F♯
and C♯).

The tenth pair of notes will be the B♭s (enharmonically A♯). The high
B♭ is fingered on the first (A) string with the left-hand index finger pad
about 1¼" from the nut. The low B♭ is fingered with the left thumb pad
on the sixth (A) string, also about 1¼" from the nut. The right middle
finger will pluck the first string at the joint, and the right thumb will
contact the sixth string at a 45° angle. While practicing, remember to use
the left-hand index finger on the high B♭. The next scale we will play is
the F-major scale (see figure 5.4), which has one flat (B♭).

The eleventh pair of notes will be the E♭s (enharmonically D♯). The
high E♭ is fingered on the third (C) string with the left-hand little finger pad about 4" from the nut. The low E♭ is fingered with the tip of
the left index finger on the fifth (D) string about 1¼" from the nut. The
left thumb will support the fingers on the back of the neck. The right
index finger will pluck the third string, and the thumb will contact the

D Major Scale
Written in standard guitarrón notation

FIGURE 5.3

F Major Scale
Written in standard guitarrón notation

Reminder: Play a pair of strings for each note.

FIGURE 5.4

fifth string at a 45° angle. The thumb must be extended outward, allowing the thumb pad to contact the string. Pull the strings toward each other in a diagonal, upward motion, bending the right wrist slightly upward and releasing the strings simultaneously. Make sure both strings are played with equal volume. Press the left-hand index and little fingers firmly.

The final note to be learned is G♯ (enharmonically A♭), which is usually performed using just one string. It is fingered on the fourth (G) string with the tip of the left index finger about 1¼" from the nut. The right thumb will pluck this low G♯, contacting the fourth string at a 45° angle. Press the left-hand index finger firmly.

The chromatic scale in figure 5.5 is a review of all twelve *guitarrón* fingerings. Practice it slowly, focusing on both the production of correct intonation and a solid, resonant tone.

A fingering chart is presented in figure 5.9, as well as musical examples in figures 5.6 through 5.9 to aid in the development of:

- Tone,
- Performing scales, and
- Flexibility.

Chromatic Scale
Written in standard guitarrón notation

Reminder: Play both strings for each note, except G#, which is played single-string.

FIGURE 5.5

Exercises for Tone Development

♩ = 96

played single-string *(una cuerda)*

played double-string

For ALL exercises: Both strings should vibrate for full duration of each note. Work for an equal volume between both strings.

Press the left hand middle finger firmly.

Press the left hand little finger firmly.

Press the left hand middle and ring fingers firmly.

Press the left thumb firmly.

Press the left hand fingertips firmly.

Press the left hand middle finger and thumb firmly.

Press the left hand fingertips firmly.

Press the left hand index finger and thumb firmly.

FIGURE 5.6

Beginner Scales and Arpeggios

FIGURE 5.7

Flexibility Exercises

FIGURE 5.8

GUITARRÓN FINGERING CHART

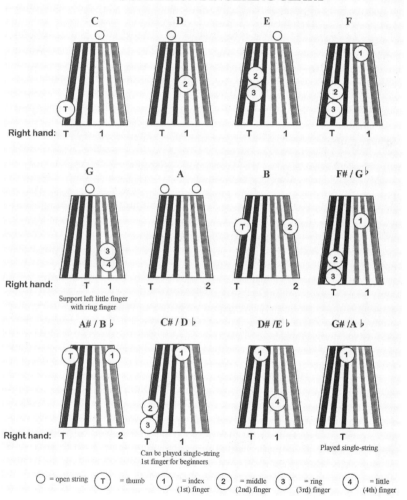

FIGURE 5.9

While this is just a brief introduction to the playing technique of the *guitarrón*, it is my hope that this material, coupled with my past experiences, will aid you in your musical knowledge of the instrument. For more in-depth study of the *guitarrón*, I recommend *The Guitarrón Book*, volume 1 (1990), by John A. Vela, available through the Mariachi Connection. I also recommend *Método Práctico de Guitarrón*, volume 1 (1983), by Natividad de Santiago González.

REFERENCES

de Santiago González, N. (1983). *Método práctico de guitarrón* (vol. 1). Montebello, CA: Mariachi Publishing.

Vela, J. A. (1990). *The guitarrón book* (vol. 1). San Antonio, TX: Southern Music.

6

Teaching the
Armonía Class

The Best Part of Your Day!

WILLIAM GRADANTE

The *armonía* section of the mariachi ensemble provides the rhythmic and harmonic foundation upon which the melodic offerings of the trumpet, violins, and voices are laid. Although the dictionary definition of *armonía* is "harmony," the mariachi *armonía* section, comprised of the *vihuela*, guitar, and *guitarra de golpe* players, performs the role of rhythm section. In some cases, the *guitarrón* and harp players are considered part of the *armonía* section, but the teaching of the latter two instruments is the subject of other chapters. Performing the role of accompanists in the mariachi ensemble, however, represents only a small part of what students do in my *armonía* classes.

Because *armonía* players are not the "melody makers" of the ensemble, some mariachi teachers "leave them to their own devices," allowing them to develop their own strumming and chording techniques while the teacher concentrates on developing the melodic skills of the violin and trumpet players. This oversight may be due to the relative lack of guitar expertise on the part of the teacher or their desire to concentrate on what they believe is most important to the ensemble: the melody.

Whatever the case may be, mariachi guitar students frequently are given short shrift when it comes to their musical education. I have on several occasions spoken with high school *armonía* players in different schools, districts, and states and discovered that many are not only unaware of the music theory–related aspects of their accompaniment playing—the inherent functional relationships between specific chords and the names of the individual notes comprising their chords—but even the names of the open strings on their instruments! It goes further: I have given professional development training to practicing mariachi instructors who *themselves* demonstrated a similar lack of awareness.

It took a number of years to impress upon my school district the educational value—even necessity—of teaching the mariachi students in homogenous classes. An especially poignant argument was that the *armonía* students, particularly the *guitarrón* and *vihuela* players, were graduating from high school with severely limited music educational options, as one cannot make college entrance auditions on *guitarrón, vihuela, guitarra de golpe*, or even mariachi guitar. Once I was permitted to teach my *armonía* players in a "guitar class," however, I was able to design a mariachi *armonía* curriculum around the development of classic guitar technique, opening a wide range of opportunities to my students. While I may be unique in my approach, I feel that it makes the teaching of the mariachi ensemble both easier and more efficient.

CLASSIC GUITAR IN THE MARIACHI CLASSROOM

The study of mariachi music in our school district has traditionally begun at the sixth-grade level and, barring conflicts with varsity athletics, ROTC, or advanced placement classes, continued through the twelfth grade. In the first three to four weeks of school, sixth-grade students are taught the basics of both music literacy and guitar performance practice. We refer to the class as guitar class and not as mariachi class and stress that the techniques presented apply to whatever specific musical styles the individual students prefer. From the moment the sixth graders arrive in my classroom, they want to know exactly when they are going to have a guitar placed in their hands. I respond that, before they are assigned a guitar, they must achieve mastery in six distinct areas of "guitar knowledge":

- Guitar parts,
- Finger names and right-hand alternation,
- Performance posture,
- Guitar care,
- Note values, and
- Note reading.

GETTING STARTED

During the first month of class, I give sixth graders a syllabus describing the kinds of things they will learn during the course of the year. More effective, however, is for me to simply perform the scales, chords, and songs that they can look forward to learning, indicating the month by which they will have mastered them. At the same time, they receive daily grades for turning in the required paperwork for our program. The students need to bring in money to purchase their textbook, along with the annual instrument rental/maintenance fee ($20 per semester) mandated by the school district. They also need to return field trip permission forms, media release forms, and the school district's instrument use form. A sample instrument use form is included at the end of this chapter (see figure 6.9), but be sure to acquire all standard forms specific to your school district.

As a matter of policy, I do not encourage parents of sixth graders to purchase their own instruments because they too often purchase an unsuitable one, such as:

- A steel-string guitar (often called an acoustic guitar),
- A guitar that is of inappropriate size, or
- A guitar whose lack of craftsmanship makes playing extremely difficult.

These guitars include ones borrowed from friends and relatives and those picked up at flea markets, pawn shops, and discount department stores. Furthermore, I advise parents to wait until the end of the year before making any significant expenditure; if the child loses interest, it is unfair to force him/her (and the teacher) to continue playing through seventh grade simply to justify the monetary investment in an instrument. Our students' families tend to be highly mobile and frequently transfer to schools where guitar instruction is not yet available. Most of our families have limited financial resources, so paying the nominal rental fee is a wise hedge against such unforeseen developments. Finally, it is not economical to purchase an undersized instrument for a sixth grader who is likely to need a better-quality, full-size guitar within a year.

Usually, a family will agree to participate in the school district instrument rental program for the first year and subsequently exercise the option to participate in our rent-to-own arrangement with a local dealer. In the meantime, the individual students, through their earnest practice and concert participation, can demonstrate to their parents that they are worthy of the financial investment that the parents are being asked to make.

In our school district, all rental fees must be spent within the current academic year and exclusively for the maintenance of existing instruments and cases or the acquisition of replacements. This rule allows the astute music educator to build a self-sustaining, functional instrument inventory while freeing up other district funds for the purchase of uniforms and supplies. In the five years since the implementation of this policy at the district level, I have been able to accumulate enough instruments that, should certain students so desire (or need), they may continue to rent one from the school district through the twelfth grade. Nearly all students, however, purchase their own instruments by the time they are promoted to the high school level.

PARTS OF THE GUITAR

Sixth-grade students are told that they are being made privy to a secret language of specialized guitar terminology from which even band, orchestra, and choir members are excluded. We can talk among ourselves about techniques and performance practices that are unique to guitarists. We create a "word wall," a large chart displaying the definitions of vocabulary words and key phrases of musical, mariachi, and guitar jargon. I begin by inviting the kids to draw a picture of their dream guitar, being as detailed as possible. I try to ease their nervousness about their perceived lack of artistic abilities by simultaneously drawing my own (intentionally?) disproportionate and awkward-looking instrument on the chalkboard. After a few moments, I hold up a classic guitar, asking the students to note specific details to add to their drawings wherever they are missing.

Beginning with the head (*cabeza*), I present the names of the guitar's various parts, with parallels drawn from the human body wherever possible. The fact that almost all of my students speak some Spanish allows this to be performed bilingually. A diagram of guitar parts is included in their textbook (*¡Échenle Con Ganas, Muchachos!* volume 1), so they can study the part names at home. For the next several weeks, I spend the first ten minutes of each class drawing a guitar on the chalkboard, following specific instructions from the students as to the location, size, and function of the various parts. I will then hold up the guitar and have individual students name each guitar part as I point to it. We follow a similar procedure to identify which students have learned the names of all of their classmates. (This helps me do the same!)

FINGER NAMES AND RIGHT-HAND ALTERNATION

Next, we name the right- and left-hand fingers. The left thumb remains numberless, as its function is to provide counterresistance to the actions of the fingers, which are numbered as follows: 1—index, 2—middle, 3—ring, 4—pinkie.

The right-hand fingers derive their names from their Spanish designations:

- *p*   "*pulgar*"   (thumb)
- *i*   "*índice*"   (index)
- *m*   "*medio*"   (middle)

- *a*   *"anular"*   (ring)
- *c*   *"chico"*   (pinkie, not used)

As few sixth graders count the verb *alternate* in their active vocabulary, we begin by adding it, along with the names of guitar parts and fingers, to our word wall. *Alternate* refers to the patterns of alternation between right-hand fingers in the performance of both scales and melodies and includes:

- *i-m*   *m-i*
- *m-a*   *a-m*
- *i-a*   *a-i*

After making a clear distinction between rest stroke (*apoyando*) and free stroke (*tirando*), students perform this alternation exercise in their laps, using their left-hand fingers as "strings." Students should ensure that their right-hand fingers do not attack the "strings" from a *perpendicular* (another word wall offering) position. Rather, they should press the string into the imaginary sound hole from a 45° angle, ending their arclike motion with the fingernails approaching the palm.

DEVELOPING A "CORRECT" POSTURE

In teaching proper sitting and standing performance posture for the guitar, a fundamental tenet is "centering," positioning the instrument in the center of the torso. In order to keep the neck/fingerboard at an angle somewhere between 30° and 45° to the floor, the left foot may be propped up with the guitar case, a student backpack, or, ideally and budget permitting, a classic guitar footstool (around $10). This means that the guitar should rest on the left rather than the right thigh.

Centering the guitar facilitates the movements of both hands in performance; provides sufficient "work space" for the guitarist, regardless of the technical demands of the music; and allows the back, arms, and shoulders to remain aligned and relaxed. The *resonating* surfaces of the guitar—the sounding board, back, and sides—may not, by definition, sit flush against the player's body. Rather, it is the edges—the *interfaces between* the sounding board, back, and sides—that rest against the top of the left thigh, the inside of the right thigh, the chest, and the right forearm.

As all bodies are unique, no single "correct" posture exists. A correct posture promotes the physical comfort of the guitarist, allowing him or her to perform for extended periods while avoiding excess strain and fatigue. Anthony Glise (1997) emphasizes that "the position of the player should remain fixed, while the instrument is arranged to suit that fixed position" (p. 4). Minor adjustments reflecting unique proportioning of an individual's body are common, such as raising the footstool for an individual with a long torso.

In general, the body should be poised, leaning into and around the guitar, not slumped behind it. It is an oversimplification to describe the body as "relaxed" since, ideally, forces and counterforces are at work in creating the numerous and varied kinds of sounds we ultimately desire. Charles Duncan (1980) discusses the principle of "functional tension" (p. 12) in describing this physical attitude of the body, while Christopher Parkening (1997) uses "focused tension" (p. 57) and Scott Tennant (1995) calls it "dynamic relaxation" (p. 6). The following general steps, adapted from Tennant's videotape *Pumping Nylon* (1997), may be followed to ascertain a "proper" positioning for each individual student:

Left hand
1. Sit up straight (with relaxed lower back) on front edge of chair.
2. Extend relaxed left arm toward floor, elbow hanging beside torso.
3. Rotate palm to face forward with hand still aligned with arm.
4. Bending only at elbow, bring hand upward, directly toward shoulder.
5. Place guitar neck in left hand between frets 5 and 7.
6. Place thumb behind fingers 1 and 2.

Right hand
7. Extend relaxed right arm toward floor, elbow hanging beside torso.
8. Form "suitcase-gripping" position with fingers.
9. Raise hand to strings, placing *p* on string 5.
10. Rest *a* on string 1, over rosette.
11. Rest *m* on string 2, over edge of rosette and sound hole.
12. Rest *i* on string 3, over sound hole.
13. *i, m,* and *a* lightly touch each other, thumb slightly left of *i*.
14. Right forearm is lowered gently to edge of lower bout, or greater curve of guitar.

I demonstrate my personal performance posture—standing and sitting, both with and without a guitar—for the students to imitate. We call it "playing air guitar." We practice the movements required in "shifting" between upper and lower positions, moving the elbow alternately toward and away from the torso, keeping the knuckles, wrist, and elbow in alignment. On our right thighs, we practice various right-hand finger alternation combinations, such as:

i-m   m-i   a-m   m-a   i-a   a-i   p-i-m-a   p-a-m-i   p-i-m-i
p-m-i-m   p-a-m-a   p-m-a-m   p-i-a-i   p-a-i-a   p-i-m-i-a-i-m-i

I explain and emphasize the importance of maintaining a gentle curvature of the right wrist with respect to possible injuries, such as carpal tunnel syndrome, reiterating that all these techniques should be mastered before guitars can be distributed. This makes the students work extra hard to perform these exercises conscientiously.

CARE OF THE GUITAR
In the process of the students' completing the school district's instrument use forms required to rent a school-owned guitar, I emphasize that students will be personally and financially responsible for its everyday

maintenance. It is appropriate, then, that we devote time to discussion of the dos and don'ts of guitar care. Students are asked to bring a handkerchief-sized piece of cloth to keep in their cases in order to wipe the instrument clean—ten to thirty seconds—after every class and at-home practice session. Here in Texas, attractive bandannas bearing the Mexican, Lone Star, or American flags are available for less than a dollar at most discount department stores. Camouflage bandannas tend to be popular as well.

I inform students that they will receive their guitars bearing new sets of strings and that, as stipulated in their rental agreement contracts, they will be required to change the strings in time for both our winter and spring concerts. As I have been able to negotiate significant discounts from large music store chains, I begin collecting string money around Thanksgiving, although students are welcome to acquire them on their own. A week or two before each concert, we remove and dispose of old strings, clean and polish the instruments, and learn how to correctly restring them. I point out that restringing alone would ordinarily cost them $15 at the local music store. Guitar knowledge is valuable!

It is now appropriate to discuss tuning procedures, although I do most of the tuning for beginners, whose ears are not always sufficiently developed. We discuss the negative effects of extreme temperatures on wooden musical instruments ("Don't leave the guitar in the trunk!" and "Don't leave the guitar out on the porch!"), applying furniture polish to its surfaces, and using steel strings. I emphasize that the case should contain, exclusively, their cleaning cloth, textbook, the *tahalí* (classic guitar strap), a pencil, and the required extra set of strings.

I also display the two or three smashed guitars that were recovered in the schoolyard after neighborhood kids "found" them while guitar students were occupied shooting hoops ("Don't leave your guitar unattended! Do leave it locked up in the instrument cabinets in the classroom!"). This unit draws to a close with my recounting the (true!) story of the former student whose insistence on carrying candy and chewing gum in his guitar case ultimately led to his horrifying discovery of a colony of cockroaches homesteading in his case. (Cases tend to remain sugar free after *that* class!)

NOTES, LINES, AND SPACES

The focus of instruction now turns to the names of the lines and spaces on the staff. We learn the names of the spaces—F-A-C-E—using the rhyming word *space* and those of the lines, E-G-B-D-F, with the sentence "Elvis' Guitar Broke Down Friday." After explaining that these nine notes are not *nearly* enough to perform all the cool songs we're going to learn in the course of the year, we attach another set of E-G-B-D-F and F-A-C-E below the staff. We finish up by adding a G above the staff. I then play the resulting seventeen natural notes in first position on the guitar fingerboard, informing the astonished students that they'll be able to do this—by memory—before *El Día de Los Muertos*, November 2.

NOTE VALUES

Each class now begins with group recitation of the names of the parts of the guitar; the names of the fingers; the fourteen steps to good posture; and the names of the lines and spaces on, above, and below the staff. We also add the names and shapes of the different types of notes and rests and their relative values to this routine. Students name and draw on the chalkboard and in their textbooks the parts of a note: the head (and its two possible shadings), the stem, and the flag. Each successive note, running from whole note through half, quarter, eighth, and sixteenth, has only one distinguishing feature—the added presence of one of these elements—stem, head color, flag, double flag. Rests are discussed simultaneously. Each type of note or rest is assigned a corresponding number of beats, running from four to two to one to one half to one fourth.

I find it helpful to teach these terms bilingually, as the Spanish designations are free of certain areas of confusion inherent in the American system. For example, students logically expect that a "whole note" should receive a "whole" beat, while a half note should receive a "half" beat. By contrast, kids can easily see that a *redonda*, a Spanish whole note, is actually round, as its name suggests. It is, in fact, the *only* note that is entirely round, with neither stem nor flag. A Spanish half note, a *blanca*, is in fact, white, just as a *negra*, a quarter note, is black. The only seemingly arbitrary naming consists of calling eighth notes *corcheas*. Sixteenth notes, logically, are *semicorcheas*:

- whole note = four beats = *redonda*
- half note = two beats = *blanca*
- quarter note = one beat = *negra*
- eighth note = one half beat = *corchea*
- sixteenth note = one quarter beat = *semicorchea*

Handclapping simple rhythms written on the chalkboard is next. If I put too simple a rhythm on the board, such as four whole notes or even sixteen quarter notes, the kids will almost immediately decide, "That's boring." So I let them make up their own, and then we get to clap them out. Inserting rests is also actively encouraged, as it involves students in the manipulation of temporal elements within measures in a given time signature. As all students are aware that no guitar will be assigned until the entire class "gets all this stuff," full clapping participation is virtually guaranteed; plus, the kids love being *asked* to get loud. As the depth and breadth of required guitar knowledge increases, students voluntarily begin to create informal peer coaching dyads, because "the sooner we all get this, the sooner we all get our guitars!" I find that class time allotted for fostering these mentoring/bonding activities is well spent.

PLACING INSTRUMENTS IN THEIR HANDS

"Big Monday" has finally arrived. The students spread out across our enormous rehearsal facility (an all-concrete, 1918 model former gymnasium with only carpet added) in order to take their examination. A solid majority of the students will usually earn grades of 100 percent in all four areas: guitar parts, guitar care, note values, and lines and spaces.

On Tuesday, I assign guitars to everyone, with the understanding that Wednesday will be for "retakes" for those who failed to earn four perfect scores.

The students' dedication through the first four weeks has paid off, as I can say, "Play me some half notes on the first string!" and they enjoy immediate success. "How about some quarter notes on the fourth string?" "Now let's do that with *i-m* alternation," and so forth. I can circulate around the room, making comments such as "Josué, please put your right hand a little bit closer to the bridge," and "Iliana, can you bring that tuning head up parallel with your smile?" and I get the responses we need.

This is a great time to ensure that the kids are performing the rest stroke properly. Following the advice of my own classic guitar teacher, Michael Dailey of Texas Wesleyan University, I tell them that each stroke has four steps:

1. The string is seated between the left corner of the right-hand fingernail and the fingertip, which is positioned at a 45° angle to the string.
2. The string is pushed downward into the sound hole without allowing any of the three finger joints to collapse.
3. The finger is pulled inward toward the palm, releasing the string to slide diagonally across the fingernail and vibrate parallel to the soundboard.
4. The finger comes to rest on the adjacent string—thus, the "rest" stroke.

I then make a simple demonstration of the much harsher, more percussive sound produced by a stroke performed with the finger placed perpendicular to the string. The instant and invariably negative reaction to the quality of this sound, even among sixth-grade novices, never fails to amaze me.

Now they want to know when they can take the guitars home to practice. So I torture them just a little longer by answering, "As soon as I see perfect performance posture all around this room. I don't want you to go home and fall into a bunch of bad habits while I'm not around to nag you!" Within two or three days I relent and send the guitars home, with the students promising they will practice thirty minutes a day. It seems to work, for a while at least, as I check the instrument cabinets every evening before I leave and find that very few guitars are ever left behind.

NOTE READING

Individual notes are learned on a string-by-string basis, beginning with string 1 (E), the thinnest and the closest to the floor when the guitar is in playing position. After learning the notes on each of the first three strings (E, B, and G), the students learn and memorize five simple melodies (see Gradante 1999). This process is then repeated using the three bass strings (D, A, and E). Everyone seems to relish the opportunity to win recognition on our prominently displayed "star chart." This indicates that they have not only performed the notes of a song correctly but, more important, did so demonstrating mastery of technical aspects, including:

Posture
- Acceptable sitting posture on front of chair
- Proper adjustment of footstool
- Proper hand, elbow, and forearm positions

Right-Hand Technique
- Seating of right-hand fingernails at 45° angle to strings
- Alternation of right-hand fingers
- Right-hand thumb playing across the top plane of bass strings
- Avoidance of collapsed tip or knuckle joints
- Appropriate exploitation of right-hand timbre zones

Left-Hand Technique
- Proper placement of left thumb behind neck
- Orientation of left-hand fingers parallel to fingerboard

- Left-hand fingers playing immediately behind frets
- Left-hand fingers contacting strings with tips rather than fleshy pads
- Position shifts achieved through forearm rather than wrist movement

By Thanksgiving break, all sixth graders are able to do the following:

- Perform the seventeen natural notes in first position, using *p* throughout the series, ascending and descending (figure 6.1)
- Perform the series using *i-m*, *m-i*, *a-m*, *m-a*, *i-a*, and *a-i* throughout
- Perform the series using *p* on strings 4–6 and *i-m* (then *m-i*, *a-m*, *m-a*, *i-a*, and *a-i*) on strings 1–3 (figure 6.2)
- Perform the series using whole, half, quarter, and eighth notes

They will also be able to perform a number of simple melodies, which in my class include the likes of "Old MacDonald," "Ode to Joy," and "B-I-N-G-O." Over half of the class will also have memorized several Christmas carols, including "Jolly Old Saint Nicholas," "Good King Wenceslas," and "Jingle Bells." Along the way, the students have encountered ledger lines and various time signatures and learned to navigate

Natural Notes in First Position

After performing above exercise using i-m, perform with m-i, a-m, m-a, i-a, and a-i
Next, perform entire exercise using only p.

FIGURE 6.1

FIGURE 6.2

through a piece, observing such conventions as repeat signs, first and second endings, *Fine, Segno, D.S. al Fine,* and *D.C. al Fine.*

LEARNING OUR FIRST CHORDS

The winter concert in mid-December marks our first foray into traditional mariachi repertoire, when we rehearse "Cielito Lindo" and "De Colores" after school with the sixth-grade violin students. As there is no need to present a sixth-grade mariachi featuring sixty-odd guitarists, I challenge only a dozen or so who have mastered all ten songs required for the concert to accompany the violinists. Having developed sufficient finger independence, strength, and dexterity through our classic guitar training regimen, these selected students have a relatively easy time learning the basic chords necessary to perform in the mariachi setting in the two weeks prior to the concert.

Those students who express disappointment at not being selected are excited to learn that we will all have the opportunity to perform in the mariachi setting by the time of our *Cinco de Mayo* concert in the spring. It is at this point that the students first realize that the *armonía* section's role in the mariachi ensemble is not all that glamorous: "Our part on 'Jingle Bells' sounds just like 'Good King Wenceslas!'" They have begun to appreciate the truly multifaceted nature of the guitar.

SECOND SEMESTER OF SIXTH GRADE

Beginning in the second semester, students learn to perform duets and trios and, before spring break, arrange their own simple duets, notating the two parts both manually and using our music-writing software. We break up into "mini-mariachis" as we perform in guitar trios ("Cielito Lindo"), quartets ("De Colores" and "Las Mañanitas"), and quintets ("Las Chiapanecas," "La Feria de las Flores," and "En Tu Día"). Each arrangement in our sixth-grade text includes melodic and harmonic lines, as well as a bass part and a chordal accompaniment. Students are assigned specific parts for each ensemble piece to ensure that they are becoming well-rounded guitarists—no one is strictly a bass player, a melody player, or a chord player.

As the year winds down, students naturally begin to separate into ability-level groups. Students are not measured against each other but are encouraged to progress at their own rate. In the nine years since I completed my ninety-six-page sixth-grade textbook (*¡Échenle Con Ganas, Muchachos!* Volume 1), no student has ever been able to perform every selection included. Instead, students may study the pieces that interest them. I provide exceptionally talented and motivated students with three selections from the state of Texas "Prescribed Music List" (PML) for the University Interscholastic League solo and ensemble competition. These are from the class III (least difficult) repertoire list and include Ferdinando Carulli's "Andante" and "Waltz," along with Julio Sagreras' "Lección 61."

Over the years, a number of sixth-grade students have received first-division (exemplary) ratings for their performance of this *high school–level* literature. This same group of ten to fifteen exceptional students is invited to form our sixth-grade guitar orchestra and will perform four- and five-part pieces, both in concert and in the competitive setting.

SEVENTH GRADE

A fundamental goal of seventh-grade guitar class is learning to perform polyphonically. That is, students will perform melodic and harmonic lines with their right-hand fingers while simultaneously providing a bass line with the thumb. This is a difficult but highly rewarding endeavor, as it forms the basis for all solo guitar playing in the coming grades. We begin with selected exercises in Sagreras' (1996) method, focusing on "Lecciones 44, 46, 48, 49, and 53." The kids make steady progress through the exercises leading up to "Lección 61," the first piece that appears on our state PML for solo and ensemble competition. Most students can perform it within the first month or so, and "Lecciones 65, 67, 68, 69, and 70," also on our PML, are undertaken in succession.

By the year's end, several seventh graders will also include in their active repertoire Tárrega's "Adelita" or "Lágrima," the anonymous "Romance," Sanz's "Españoleta," or Carcassi's "Allegro, Opus 60, Number 7," all of which are class II (intermediate) solos.

At the same time, we begin each class with expanded scale study, beginning with C and G major. I discuss the seven scale degrees and the role of key signatures in maintaining the whole-step/half-step intervallic pattern that characterizes the major scale. I've never had a class where no student asked: "Well, what would happen if we *changed* the whole-whole-half-whole-whole-whole-half step pattern?" And that's great, because it leads quite conveniently to the concept of minor keys. So I introduce the relative natural, harmonic, and melodic minor scales. This means each class now begins with the kids naming, defining, and performing scales (figure 6.3) along with associated arpeggio (word wall!) exercises (see figure 6.4):

- C major
- A natural minor
- A harmonic minor
- A melodic minor
- G major
- E natural minor
- E harmonic minor
- E melodic minor

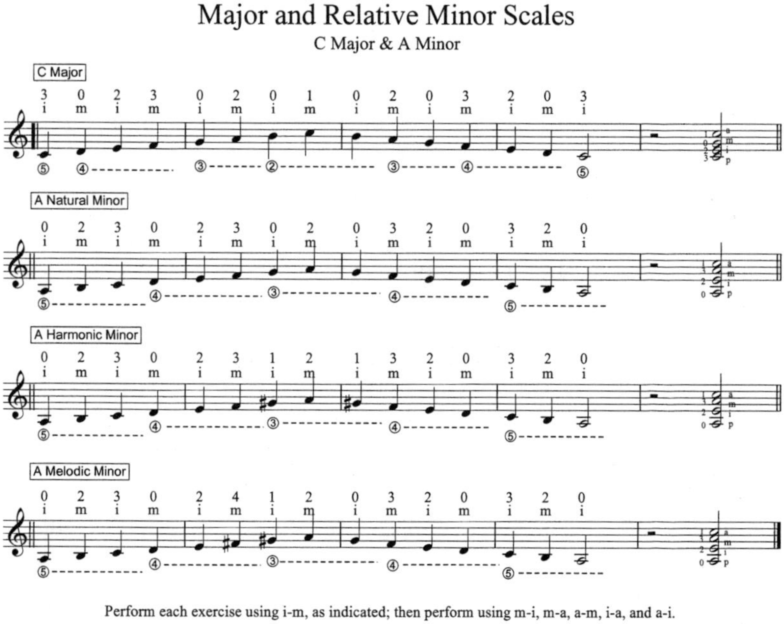
Major and Relative Minor Scales
C Major & A Minor
C Major
A Natural Minor
A Harmonic Minor
A Melodic Minor
Perform each exercise using i-m, as indicated; then perform using m-i, m-a, a-m, i-a, and a-i.

FIGURE 6.3

Daily drilling helps the students remember when to raise or lower the sixth and seventh degrees of specific scales and recognize the resulting differences between "ascending" and "descending" minor scales (word wall, again). The concept of "primary chords," those built upon the first, fourth, and fifth degrees of the scale, is next.

When one examines the repertoire of any mariachi ensemble, the existence of several genres of mariachi music becomes evident. The easiest way to distinguish these genres is by the specific *mánico* (strumming pattern) employed by the *armonía* players. These genres/*mánicos*, listed in the approximate order of their introduction, include those found in table 6.1. This has an enormous effect upon the manner in which you can teach your classes. In order to perform their traditional role in the mariachi ensemble, the *armonía* players must learn to play chords. I have had best success

FIGURE 6.4

Table 6.1. **Pedagogical Sequence for** *Armonía Mánicos*

Grade 6		
	Bolero	4/4
	Ranchera valseada	3/4
	Ranchera lenta	4/4
	Cumbia	2/4
Grade 7		
	Danza habanera	4/4
	Danzón	4/4
	Ranchera (polqueada)	2/4
	Polka	2/4
	Bolero ranchero	4/4
	Bolero guapachoso	4/4
Grade 8		
	Pasodoble	4/4
	*Jarabe*6/8>	
	Son jalisciense	3/4 (6/8)
	Huapango/Son huasteco	3/4 (6/8)
	Joropo	3/4 (6/8)

Basic Mánicos for Armonías

FIGURE 6.5
(*continues*)

teaching these one key at a time, reinforcing the I–IV–V⁷–I model, and proceeding in the following order, as they become increasingly challenging:

- A major (sixth grade)
- D major (sixth grade)
- G major (sixth grade)

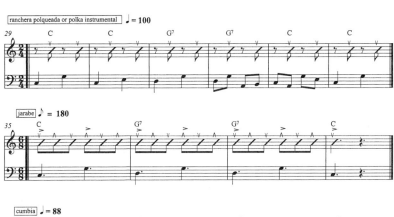

FIGURE 6.5
(*continued*)

- C major (seventh grade)
- E major (seventh grade)
- F major (seventh grade)
- B♭ major (eighth grade)
- E♭ major (eighth grade)

Son Jalisciense
Frequently Encountered Mánicos

The various *mánicos* presented above may be encountered in any number of different patterns within a given *son jalisciense*.

FIGURE 6.6

Son Huasteco or Huapango
Frequently Encountered Mánicos

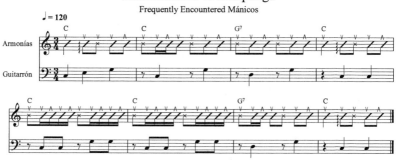

FIGURE 6.7

Joropo
Frequently Encountered Mánicos

FIGURE 6.8

In the sixth grade, the students had some experience performing in the mariachi context: the winter concert, the spring concert, recruiting concerts at elementary schools, and our local mariachi competition. They developed basic competency in performing the primary chords in A major, D major, and G major but now require a more systematic approach. We utilize a student-generated rubric to evaluate and reward student progress toward what we call "key mastery." The consensus of a recent group of seventh graders was that, in order to claim "mastery" of chordal performance in any given key, the student would have to demonstrate the following:

- The ability to name the three primary chords in the key
- The correct fingering of each chord
- Making all six chord changes (I–V^7, V^7–I, I–IV, IV–I, IV–V^7, V^7–IV)
- Making all six chord changes in rhythm (no pauses)
- Making changes with fingers *jumping* into position (no walking)
- Proper right-hand wrist strumming (no forearm action)
- Clear sound production (no buzzing)
- Sight-reading a piece in the given key (the "mastery song")

My seventh-grade textbook (*¡Échenle Con Ganas, Muchachos!* volume 2) includes all of the appropriate chord fingering charts, coordinated with exercises designed to prepare the student to fulfill these requirements. In generating their own rubric, students gained a sense of ownership of the learning process and became clearly aware of the specific concepts and skills they are expected to master. When seventh graders feel ready to demonstrate mastery of a given key, they can perform the required test: sight-reading a previously unknown piece of music while referring to the posted rubric and then telling me *themselves* which standards they feel they have mastered and which require further practice.

Armed with a clear grasp of the educational "destination," most students grade themselves far more harshly than I *ever* would. There are no trick questions, no curveballs, no surprises, and no disappointments.

Performance standards and assessments are aligned. The students' reward is that they are now capable of performing that "mastery song" they've been longing to play. *My* reward is the mad rush by their classmates to demonstrate *their own* mastery of these standards so that *they* get to play that song, too. Most gratifying is that the students learn skills and concepts, apply them in performance, analyze the "mastery song's" challenges, synthesize the solution, and end with self-evaluation.

LEARNING THE *MÁNICOS*

As a rule, the young guitarist faced with the challenge of performing chords encounters difficulty due to lack of three things: finger independence, strength, and flexibility. When chord playing is introduced after the student has received basic classic guitar training, these crucial elements are largely in place. Daily scale work, along with arpeggio exercises in seventh and eighth grade, makes chord playing a logical next step from what they've already been doing. Clumsy finger movements, collapsing finger joints, and weak-sounding chords become nonissues.

Sixth-grade repertoire concentrates on genres featuring mostly downward strumming, such as in the *rancheras* and *bolero*. In seventh grade, we can add the simple *redoble* figures (two eighth notes followed by one or two quarter notes) simply by learning to strum upward. Fingers should not be thrown across the strings, separating from the thumb, but should remain in gentle but constant contact with it. The upstroke is simply a return to the starting position, with the thumbnail striking the strings from 1 through 6. We concentrate on smooth wrist rotation and use of a straight and powerful right thumb. Forearm movement is limited to rotation of the ulna and radius bones; swinging from the elbow is strongly discouraged, at least until they make their first video for MTV!

Every so often I will spend half an hour or so teaching in the time-tested fashion of "oral tradition." I will strum a measure or two and, without any speaking permitted, challenge the students to imitate the rhythmic pattern, internalizing the *mánico*. I call this "getting in shape," as it eventually becomes a test of endurance. I generally stand, facing the class in mariachi performance posture. As the students tire, I can always point out that "I'm an old guy" and have been "sweet" enough to allow them to remain seated. This, of course, prompts the "hotshots" to leap to their feet to meet my thinly veiled challenge with renewed vitality. We remain on the same chord for quite a while, encouraging the kids to concentrate solely on right-hand issues, interspersing muscle relaxation and stretching exercises at regular intervals.

The only remaining technique is the *golpe apagado* or *apagón*. It is rather simple to perform as long as the wrist and forearm remain relaxed. Everybody, including sixth graders, seems to want to learn to play "El Mariachi Loco" and will enthusiastically make the extra effort to learn to make the *apagón*. Written with an X-shaped note head, the *apagón* consists of a downward strum in which the vibrating strings are damped immediately after being struck by the fingers.

This is one of the very few instances in which the right-hand wrist will cease to arch outward away from the strings; instead, it thrusts inward, pushing the heel of the hand onto the strings, resulting in a pleasantly percussive *chick*-ing sound. A mainstay of the *cumbia*, the *apagón* also figures prominently in the *mánicos* of the *joropo, bolero ranchero*, and each of the several variant *huapango* forms. Featured in the *joropo*, the upward *apagón* creates a similar effect by damping the strings with the lowered, outside edges of the upstroking fingers (see figures 6.5–6.8).

"WHAT ELSE CAN YOU GET SEVENTH GRADERS TO DO?"

During the course of the seventh grade, *armonía* students perform polyphonic solos in concert and competition, participate monophonically in our guitar orchestra, and join our violinists in the mariachi setting, providing chordal accompaniment. In addition, I address our state-mandated Texas Essential Knowledge and Skills criteria regarding the cultural and historical aspects of mariachi music by including instructional units on the following topics:

- *16 de Septiembre* (Mexican Independence Day)
- *El Día de los Muertos* (The Day of the Dead)
- *Cinco de Mayo* (The Fifth of May)
- José Alfredo Jiménez, mariachi singer/songwriter
- Jorge Negrete/Pedro Infante/Javier Solís/Miguel Aceves Mejía, mariachi icons
- Mariachi history

As the mariachi ensemble is a highly sought-after subject of local media interest, with newspapers, radio stations, and television reporters having done stories on our program, it behooves us to prepare our students for the inevitable questions they will have to field:

- "What does *El 16 de Septiembre* mean to you as a Hispanic American?"
- "How do you feel when you perform on *El Día de los Muertos?*"
- "What does the word *mariachi* mean?"
- "Tell us about your costume."
- "What do you call the big, fat guitar, and where does it come from?"
- "What happened on *Cinco de Mayo?*"
- "What do you like about playing mariachi music?"

Furthermore, the growing self-esteem and cultural awareness that our students derive from this sort of study is made manifest in both their stage presence and in the basic attitude they adopt in their daily lives.

Clearly, making an effort to link in-school activities with the greater community can be highly beneficial to your mariachi program. In most communities, outstanding cultural organizations exist that are delighted to network with local schools. We have been the beneficiaries of the generosity of our local classic guitar society, Guitar Fort Worth (www.guitarfortworth.org), having been invited on a regular basis to attend both master classes and public concerts presented by international recording artists, *all free of charge.*

These artists are brought right to our school where they perform and present master classes, listening to, advising, and encouraging individual students. For the artists, it is exciting (sometimes astonishing and overwhelming) to see such a large group of students so deeply involved in serious guitar study. For us, it's almost like we're staging our own private "career day" for guitar students. While such major activities take place only four or five times a year, in conjunction with the ongoing concert series, Guitar Fort Worth has also arranged for several guitar majors at local universities to visit our classroom to work on a weekly basis with my students, providing both mentoring and role models for our future artists.

Both our seventh- and eighth-grade curricula include instruction in *guitarrón, guitarra de golpe,* and *vihuela* performance. As I have been able to accumulate fifteen *vihuelas* and seventeen *guitarrones,* specific class days are devoted to group instruction on these instruments. "Specialization," however, is not encouraged at this time. That is, in a given performance, a student may perform as a mariachi guitarist but must move to *vihuela* or *guitarrón,* for example, for our next outing. More often, students choose to perform certain songs on *guitarrón* and others on guitar, *guitarra de golpe,* or *vihuela,* within the context of a single performance. My goal is to keep everyone well rounded. Students are not permitted to abandon the development of their classic guitar repertoire, but so far, no one has ever expressed that desire.

EIGHTH GRADE

The purpose of eighth-grade guitar class is to enable the students to sight-read virtually any piece of music that might be placed upon their stand once they arrive at the high school mariachi class. In addition, they will have developed the classic guitar technical skills needed to perform a number of class I (advanced) or class II (intermediate) selections from the PML. As in grade 7, we begin the eighth-grade year listening to recordings of a number of both mariachi and PML selections, so that the students can choose pieces that they especially enjoy and get started preparing them for performance and competition. We review the previous year's mariachi ensemble and guitar orchestra repertoire, making appropriate changes in the arrangements so they match the current level of student competence.

In addition, we get considerably more sophisticated in our study of music theory, as students relate their daily scale work with the concept of primary and secondary chords. Secondary chords, minor chords built on the second and sixth degrees of the scale, are combined with the tonic and dominant seventh chords to form *círculos* ("circles"). As they have already performed the G-major *círculo* playing simple *boleros* like "Cariño" in the mariachi context, the concept is easily understood: "We are learning to play 'Cariño' in eight different keys!"

Now every class begins with the performance of the *círculos* in each of the major keys listed previously. I ask, "Which key has *x* number of sharps (or flats)?" and the students respond with the name of the key and the names of the sharped (or flatted) notes and perform the appropriate *círculo*, upholding the standards established in the seventh-grade rubric. Once the primary (I, IV, and V^7) and secondary (I, vi, ii^7, and V^7) chords in the eight specified keys are mastered and memorized, all that remains for the *armonía* player is to learn and internalize the various strumming patterns enumerated earlier and then combine the two. Sixth graders have little trouble performing the *bolero* or the various *ranchera mánicos*, and seventh graders drill on the polka, *ranchera polqueada, danzón, bolero ranchero*, and *danza habanera*. This leaves the *pasodoble, son jalisciense* (and its several variant forms), *jarabe, huapango/son huasteco*, and *joropo* for the eighth grade.

Meanwhile, the melody instruments must learn and master their scales and apply them to the individual pieces being studied, a very labor-intensive and time-consuming task. The key point here is that, while each subsequent song studied by the trumpet and violin players will present new melodies and associated articulation, expression, and intonation challenges, the *mánicos*, chording requirements, and even general *guitarrón* patterns remain constant for *armonía* players. These students must simply master their keys and apply the various *mánicos* in daily exercises, a relatively simple and straightforward process.

In almost thirty years of teaching middle school, high school, and college student mariachis, I have found that, in a heterogeneous class, the *armonía* players tend to spend a lot of time sitting around the rehearsal hall killing time, waiting for the melody players to "catch up." The instructor must either ask them to wait quietly while he entreats the melody players to "articulate that correctly," "play it in tune," or "fix those bowings" or be resigned to simply run through the repertoire, ignoring obvious errors, just to keep the guitarists involved and "on task." This holds true in the classroom setting as well as in the context of the numerous mariachi conferences we have attended.

For this reason, I feel that the *armonía* students are best served in a homogenous classroom as long as possible, where I can continue teaching the full spectrum of guitar performance that they will need at the next level of their musical education. Since your students are likely to have regularly scheduled, after-hours varsity and junior varsity rehearsals anyway, why not teach the sections separately during school hours and, thus, maximize time on task?

CONCLUSIONS

If it seems that the incoming ninth-grade *armonía* players are pretty much ready to "spread their wings and fly" through the high school mariachi curriculum, it's because that's been our plan since the sixth grade. My point all along has been that it is our duty to push our *armonía* players to reach their fullest potential, preparing them for future success better than we have in the past. High school, then, gives them time to expand their repertoire and master the increasingly complex techniques required in its performance.

"Standards," repertoire elements every mariachi or classic guitarist ought to know, should take precedence, not the hottest new tune kids hear through the mass media. Students should be shown the importance of learning pieces of both mariachi and classic guitar literature representing different eras, styles, and composers. I would no more want my classic guitarists to be able to perform only compositions by Francisco Tárrega than I would like my mariachis to perform concerts of only *rancheras* or *boleros* they've heard sung by Luís Miguel.

While most of the *mánicos* and chord knowledge required for mariachi music performance can be learned by the end of eighth grade, our high school guitar students find that, as they approach intermediate and advanced classic guitar literature, a number of techniques still wait to challenge them. It is, however, far beyond the scope of this chapter to discuss them all here. They are addressed in great detail and with great skill in many of the publications listed in the bibliography and are only briefly mentioned in the following:

- Scale Study: Scales studied at the middle school level in only one or two octaves should be expanded to two or three octaves. These should include the following major scales along with their three relative minor scales: C, G, D, A, E, F, B♭, and E♭ (the same as in primary and secondary chord studies). My own guitar teacher Michael Dailey states that were he abandoned on a desert island with only one book to maintain his guitar technical skills, it would be Andrés Segovia's (1953) booklet of scale studies.
- Arpeggios: Tennant (1995) contains all of Mauro Giuliani's 120 right-hand exercises. Ablóniz (1954) and Hamilton and McFadden (2004) approach arpeggio study in a very systematic manner. The full gamut of Giuliani's pedagogical materials is found in Giuliani (1995). The key concept of "planting" is discussed in Tennant (1995[QU5]), Glise (1997), and Barreiro (2002).
- General Technique: A number of technical problems presented to the performer of both intermediate and advanced guitarists are dealt with in most of the "Method Books" as well as the "Studies for Technical Development" listed in the bibliography of this chapter, including:

barres, partial barres, and hinge barres; playing beyond fret 12; true and artificial harmonics; ascending and descending slurs; mordents and trills; vibrato; pivot and guide fingers; tremolo; *rasgueado*; *tambor*; and so on.

- Interpretation: The concepts of timbre, tempo, and volume and their importance in the performance of guitar literature with expression and artistry cannot be overstated. Publications listed under "Guitar Pedagogy" and "Repertoire Development" are highly recommended.

In closing, I hope it has become clear that there is absolutely no reason structuring and teaching the *armonía* class should be something to be dreaded or, worse, left to the students themselves, as is currently too often the case. Rather, it can easily be the most exciting part of teaching mariachi at your school. The versatility of the guitar itself, coupled with the enormous appetite of your students to devour music of all styles, eras, and genres, can hardly fail to consistently provide you with the high point in your teaching day. It has for me for over half of my life! *¡Échenle con ganas, Muchachos!*

BIBLIOGRAPHY OF CLASSIC GUITAR SOURCES TO CONSULT

Method Books

Barreiro, E. (2002). *Introduction to classical guitar.* Pacific, MO: Mel Bay.

Carcassi, M. (1994). *The complete Carcassi guitar method* (J. Castle, ed.). Pacific, MO: Mel Bay.

Carulli, F. (1955, 1983). *Método completo per chitarra.* Milan: Casa Ricordi Editore.

Gradante, W. J. (1999). *"¡Échenle con ganas, muchachos!": A mariachi textbook* (*armonías* vols. 1–3). Available from the author.

Mills, J. (1981). *The classical guitar tutor.* London: Musical New Services.

Noad, F. M. (1972). *Playing the guitar: A self-instruction guide to technique and theory* (Revised 3rd ed.). New York: G. Schirmer.

Noad, F. M. (1978). *First book for the guitar.* Milwaukee: Hal Leonard.

Sagreras, J. (1996). *Lecciones de guitarra* (books 1–3). Pacific, MO: Mel Bay. (Spanish-English).

Shearer, A. (1969). *Classic guitar technique* (vols. 1–2). Van Nuys, CA: Belwin Mills.

Tennant, S. (2003). *Basic classical guitar method* (book 1). Van Nuys, CA: Alfred.

Tennant, S. (2004). *Basic classical guitar method* (book 2). Van Nuys, CA: Alfred.

Studies for Technical Development

Ablóniz, M. (1954). *Arpeggi per la mano destra, per chitarra.* Ancona, Italy: Berben Edizioni Musicale.

Giuliani, M. (1995). *Complete Giuliani studies* (D. Grimes, ed.). Pacific, MO: Mel Bay.

Pujol, E. (1983). *Guitar school: A theoretical-practical method for the guitar, based on the principles of Francisco Tárrega* (English ed.). Columbus, OH: Editions Orpheé.

Segovia, A. (1953). *Diatonic major and minor scales.* Washington, DC: Columbia Music.

Sor, F. (1994). *Complete Sor studies* (D. Grimes, ed.). Pacific, MO: Mel Bay.

Tennant, S. (1995). *Pumping nylon: A guide to classical guitar technique.* Van Nuys, CA: Alfred.

Tennant, S. (1997). *Pumping nylon: A guide to classical guitar technique* [Motion picture]. United States: Alfred.

Repertoire Development

Hamilton, R., and McFadden, J. (2004). *Guitar series: Guitar repertoire and studies/etudes* (3rd ed., vols. 1–8). Toronto: Frederick Harris Music.

Noad, F. (1974–1986). *The Frederick Noad guitar anthology* (books 1–4: The baroque guitar, The classical guitar, The renaissance guitar, The romantic guitar.) New York: Ariel Music.

Parkening, C. (1997). *The Christopher Parkening guitar method: The art and technique of the classical guitar* (vol. 2). Milwaukee: Hal Leonard.

Parkening, C. (1999). *The Christopher Parkening guitar method: The art and technique of the classical guitar* (Revised ed., vol. 1). Milwaukee: Hal Leonard.

Tennant, S. (1998). *Pumping nylon: Supplemental repertoire for the best-selling classical guitarist's technique handbook (easy to early intermediate).* Van Nuys, CA: Alfred.

Tennant, S. (1999). *Pumping nylon: Supplemental repertoire for the best-selling classical guitarist's technique handbook (intermediate to advanced).* Van Nuys, CA: Alfred.

Guitar Pedagogy

Duncan, C. (1980). *The art of classical guitar playing* (books 1–3). Miami: Summy-Birchard.

Glise, A. (1997). *Classical guitar pedagogy: A handbook for teachers.* Pacific, MO: Mel Bay.

Shearer, A. (1990). *Learning the classic guitar* (vols. 1–3). Pacific, MO: Mel Bay.

Fort Worth Independent School District
Instrumental Music Programs

AGREEMENT FOR USE OF MUSICAL INSTRUMENT

The parent and the student request that the student be allowed to use, and the School District agrees to allow the use of, the following described instrument for a maintenance fee of $20 per semester for secondary students and $10 per semester for elementary students:

Instrument _____ Make_____ Model _____ Serial Number _____

Together with the following accessories:
_____Bow _____Bag _____Case _____Shoulder Rest _____Mouthpiece

Additional accessories: _____

Condition of instrument: _____

In consideration of the use of the instrument, said parent and student agree that:

1. The student/parent(s) agree to pay the annual instrument maintenance fee
2. The student will practice diligently according to the instructions of the music teacher
3. The student will play in public functions when requested to do so by the music teacher
4. The parent(s) and the student will be personally responsible for any damage to, or the loss of, this instrument while in the student's care. If the instrument is lost or damaged beyond repair the parent(s) and/or student will pay the School District the cost of replacing it with one of the same make or of equal quality
5. The parent(s) and the student will return this instrument upon request of the music teacher, in as good condition as received, ordinary wear and depreciation excepted

Under no condition should parent(s)/student attempt to make repairs on instrument

It is further understood that said pupil is to replace such items as strings and reeds for loaned instrument as needed.

This agreement ends _____, and the instrument must be returned by this date.

Campus/School Name   Parent/Guardian Signature & Date

Student Name/ID#   Address

Student Signature & Date   **Driver's License Number**

Name/Address/Phone Number of Nearest Relative NOT living with you

Date Paid - Fall Semester   Date Paid-Spring Semester

Date Returned   Band/Orchestra Director Signature & Date

Notes:_____

White – School Copy   Pink- Student Copy   Yellow – Music Office Copy

FIGURE 6.9

7

Teaching the Mariachi Violin Section

Mack Ruiz

The responsibilities of teaching the mariachi violin section are similar to those of teaching an orchestra or strings program. Your mariachi string curriculum should be well planned and sequential. As the mariachi strings teacher, your understanding of the national standards affects the success of your program. MENC's publication *Strategies for Teaching Strings and Orchestra*, available at www.menc.org/orchestra, demonstrates how national standards relate to the instructional process through detailed lesson planning. Teaching strategies and lesson plans outlined in this publication can be adapted to your mariachi string instruction.

As important as national standards are in telling us what every student should know and be able to do, standards are equally important for the teacher. The American String Teachers Association (ASTA), dedicated to string pedagogy and playing, has established the following string teaching standards. Like most standards, they are voluntary in nature, imply what string teachers should know and be able to do, and may be adapted for use within the mariachi teaching realm.

STRING TEACHING STANDARDS

As an educator, you should:

- understand and apply pedagogy for violin;
- demonstrate effective rehearsal techniques;
- demonstrate the knowledge of repertoire for student performance;
- demonstrate skill in arranging music;
- demonstrate strategies for integrating music with other disciplines;
- understand different student learning styles, levels of maturation, and special needs and adapt instruction accordingly;
- demonstrate knowledge of comprehensive, sequential K–12 music curricula;
- demonstrate understanding of the principles of a variety of homogeneous and heterogeneous pedagogical approaches for teaching string classes;
- demonstrate effective methods of assessing and evaluating student achievement;
- know about instrument rental and purchasing;
- know current technology for instruction, research, and musical applications;
- demonstrate the ability to develop budgets for equipment and supplies; and
- demonstrate an understanding of the K–12 National Music Education Standards and other state and local standards for music.

For a full list of standards, see www.astaweb.com.

The challenges that face string teaching in our public school systems are the lack of strings programs, the lack of string instructors, and the lack of support for string programs. Today, string programs exist in only 35 percent of our elementary schools, 19 percent of our middle schools, and 31 percent of our high schools. According to ASTA, only one in every five students currently has access to strings programs in our public schools. Because of this, middle school and high school mariachi programs are often faced with the challenge of teaching basic instrument fundamentals to their students.

One thing is certain: Fundamental violin pedagogy is essential for your mariachi violin students. Your lesson planning must supply them with violin pedagogy that is well planned and sequential in nature. When it comes to repertoire, you must select pieces that are within the range of your students' achievement levels.

In observing mariachi school groups, particularly their violin sections, the most noticeable weaknesses are in the (1) fundamental violin technique and (2) ensemble performance. As a mariachi instructor, your responsibility to continually review the mechanics and techniques of violin performance will keep your students in check. Portion periods of time into your lesson planning to cover the following.

BASIC VIOLIN FUNDAMENTALS TO REVIEW

- Posture
- Bow Hold
- Straight Bow Geometry
- The Fundamental *Detaché* Bow Stroke

Posture

One of the most corrected fundamentals in young players is imbalanced posture. Posture helps to establish a foundation for violin performance. Signs of good posture include the following:

- If the student is standing, the feet should be shoulder-width apart.
- The back should be erect, and the weight of the body should be centered.
- The violin should be under the chin and positioned horizontally.

Many students may use a shoulder rest, depending on the length of the neck or body type. In cases where the student's neck is very short, the use of a shoulder rest may not be advised.

Bow Hold

Even though students may be able to demonstrate a classic bow hold, they may tend to lose the hold in the middle of a bow stroke. Make sure to check their bow holds often for correctness. A consistent bow hold will help them achieve straight bowing. Bow hold fundamentals include the following:

- Place the right thumb on the inside part of the bow where the frog curves.
- Position the three middle fingers on the outside of the bow.
- Position the pinkie on top, close to the adjustment screw.
- Position the side of your index finger on the bow hold.

For more information on bow hold and any of the following subjects, consult www.violinmasterclass.com.

Straight Bow Geometry

Simply telling your students to keep the bow straight isn't enough. To begin with, no natural body motion allows the bow to travel in a straight line. The straight bow stroke requires that the upper arm, wrist, and elbow make adjustments that allow the bow to travel parallel to the bridge. In the straight bow stroke, certain geometrical principles are apparent. Try to imagine the violin in position with the bow on the string (1) at the middle of the bow, (2) at the tip of the bow, and (3) at the frog of the bow.

1. Middle of the bow—When the bow stroke is passing through the middle of the bow, a square should form between the sounding point (where the bow lies on the string), the shoulder, the elbow, and the hand.
2. Tip of the bow—When the bow stroke is at the tip of the bow, a triangle should form between the shoulder, the hand, and the sounding point.

3. Frog of the bow—When the bow stroke approaches the frog of the bow, a triangle should form between the shoulder, the elbow, and the hand.

To help the student to visualize the principles of straight bowing, a mirror is useful:

- Have your student stand sideways to the mirror to view bow direction.
- On a down bow, push your elbow forward to keep the bow straight at the tip.
- On an up bow, pull the elbow back as you approach the middle to the frog of the bow.

The Fundamental *Detaché* Stroke

Students who have been playing for years often fail to consistently demonstrate good or excellent control of the *detaché* stroke, which is one of the most important bow motions. *Detaché* is a French word referring to the motion of smooth, separate bowings for each note played. In English, it does not mean "detached" or "disconnected." The *detaché* stroke is used in playing successions of notes that are of equal value. A bow lift is not used at the end of the *detaché* stroke to change direction.

Once your students improve their *detaché* stroke, they will improve general bow control, sound projection, and sound consistency in their performance. Characteristics of the *detaché* bow stroke include the following:

- It is usually performed in the upper half of the bow but can be used closer to the frog or as a whole bow stroke.
- Notes are played with a constant bow pressure and speed.
- Notes are of equal value and bow length.

The *detaché* exercises in figures 7.1 and 7.2 may be practiced with the use of pieces, such as the classic Kreutzer Etude no. 2 or excerpts from

FIGURE 7.1
"El Tranchete"—son jalisciense

mariachi pieces like those in figures 7.1 and 7.2. Instructions for both
exercises are:

- Set a metronome to a very slow speed.
- Play using the upper half to the middle of the bow.
- Maintain the bow in a straight motion so that the sounding point does
  not change.
- On the down bow, move the elbow forward.
- On the up bow, bring the elbow in.
- Check your bow hold often to keep it consistent.

FIGURE 7.2
"Paloma Sin Nido"—ranchera

Continually check your students' bow strokes and make corrections as needed. Students should strive to achieve clear, concise articulation. When your violin section becomes well versed at this stroke and others, they will take steps toward better articulation in their ensemble performance.

ENSEMBLE TECHNIQUES

Vital to successful ensemble performance of the mariachi violin section is its ability to take musical direction from its section leader as well as from other focal points in the mariachi ensemble. In the orchestral realm, the conductor communicates musical directives to the principals of various sections and their musicians through the use of a baton. The mariachi ensemble shares similar characteristics in that it is an orchestra with its own instrumental sections and principals, but the mariachi ensemble must operate without a conductor. Unable to receive directives through the use of a baton in a performance, the mariachi musician must rely upon more subtle indicators for musical direction. Thus, the use of body movement, eye contact, facial gestures, and breathing become essential for communication in this particular ensemble.

Dr. Lorenzo Francisco Candelaria, professor of musicology at the University of Texas at Austin, suggested that Mariachi Cobre take a systematic approach to mariachi ensemble performance through the use of "focal points." He stated that

> once a focal point, the section leader or principal, has been established for each section, it becomes the responsibility of each remaining member to focus his/her attention on the section leader. These three focal points are responsible for staying together with one another, and their respective sections are responsible for staying together with them, even in the cases where the principals are slightly off. (Candelaria, 1996)

The three main focal points of the mariachi may well be the lead violin, the *guitarrón* player, and the lead trumpet. Through time, if these three section leaders, or focal points, can act as a single entity, playing off one another, they will serve as a center point or musical reference for the musicians surrounding them. In the violin section, establishing a musical hierarchy of sorts allows its members to closely follow the cues, bowings, and fingerings of the principal violinist.

MUSICAL CUES

We have all heard some form of the phrase, "the ensemble that breathes together plays together." Though most associate it with wind players, violin and other sections of the mariachi may find breathing an important aspect of starting pieces and phrases. Here, the lead violinist may use a breath accompanied by an angular downbeat, using the scroll of the violin. For example, a slow *bolero* in 4/4 time, entering on beat 1, may be cued by counting/tapping three quarter notes followed by a quarter-note breath coupled with placement of the bow, in a relaxed circular motion on the string and using the scroll of the violin to give an angular downbeat. A polka in 2/4 time, entering on beat 1, may be cued by counting one quarter note followed by a short expressive quarter-note breath, coupled with a sharp angular downbeat.

Whether using a count coupled with a gesture or simply giving an angular downbeat as used for certain 3/4 and 6/8 *sones jaliscienses*, the cue should always be given in the spirit of the piece that you are about to play. Remember, musicians tend to respond to the intensity of cues and gestures.

BOWING

For a string section to paint the same musical landscape, it is important for each musician to paint with the same stroke. Violin ensemble performance requires the same bow division and bow stroke. It only takes one violinist to change the tonal quality of the section by using a different bow approach.

The sounding point or the section of the string used to play upon is also of importance. The closer you play to the bridge, the brighter the timbre produced. As the sounding point moves closer to the middle and upward toward the fingerboard, the timbre changes to a rounder, then softer sound. All violinists of the mariachi should closely replicate the bow division and bow placement of the principal in a performance. As an instructor, ensure that each of your students is well versed in the various bow strokes and techniques required by music in your repertoire.

FINGERING AND USE OF VIBRATO

The violin section should strive to use the same or similar fingerings and vibratos so that tonal qualities within the section remain the same. If your students are beginning or intermediate students, they are likely to be accustomed to playing in only the first or the first and third positions. Choose music and fingerings that are appropriate for them. As their students' technique develops, however, it becomes essential for teachers to challenge students by introducing higher positions. In preparing for studies of higher positions, review the basic fundamentals for shifting:

- Keep the finger(s) in contact with the string while shifting up and down.
- The thumb should always shift with the fingers.
- Maintain the finger shape and the hand shape throughout the shift.

Vibrato requires varying the speed (oscillations) for certain pieces. For example, a *son jalisciense* in 3/4 may require the use of a faster vibrato (or in some cases, very little vibrato at all), whereas a *bolero* in 4/4 time may call for a slower, wider, and more intense vibrato. The two most practical forms of the vibrato are the arm (or forearm) vibrato and the hand (or wrist) vibrato.

- Arm vibrato—The forearm rapidly moves backward and forward; the wrist does not flex.
- Hand vibrato—The forearm remains still; the wrist moves backward and forward.

Since vibrato's purpose is to intensify and enhance musical expression through its technical movements, all members of the section should try to duplicate the expressions of the principal by duplicating the vibrato, thus painting the same musical landscape. For additional vibrato resources, see *Essential Technique for Strings, Intermediate Technique Studies*, published by Hal Leonard (Allen, Gillespie, and Tellejohn Hayes, 1997). For vibrato information and all other pedagogical matters, I highly recommend www.violinmasterclass.com.

As a mariachi educator, you are a strings teacher. The time that you spend researching the various resources currently available for string pedagogy is time well spent. If you are an active member of MENC, ASTA, or one of the many associations advocating the teaching of the arts, access to resources is critical. Through your membership with MENC Mariachi, learn how you may support your own program and mariachi programming nationally.

REFERENCES

Allen, M., Gillespie, R., and Tellejohn Hayes, P. (1997). Essential technique for strings, intermediate technique studies. Milwaukee: Hall Leonard.

Candelaria, L. (1996). Personal communication.

8

Teaching Trumpet Technique to Mariachi Students

NOÉ SÁNCHEZ, STEVE CARRILLO, AND
WILLIAM GRADANTE

As is true for any instrumental music student, mariachi trumpet players require a systematic program of instruction in all aspects of their instrument. However, due to the inherent differences in the educational policies and philosophies of individual school districts, administrators, and the teachers themselves, this may take any of a number of forms.

In some school districts, mariachi trumpet players may be required to participate in the band program. This may be due to the relative size of the band or mariachi programs or be a function of school district budgetary restraints. However, this should not present a problem for the mariachi instructor, as long as the relationship between the band program and the mariachi program is one characterized by cooperation rather than by competition, mutual distrust, or exclusivity. This, of course, applies in equal measure to the relationships cultivated between the mariachi program and the school's respective orchestra and choir programs, especially if students are to be similarly "shared."

Trumpet instruction at the developmental level should be largely the same whether the ultimate goal is to perform band or mariachi repertoire. Certainly, all trumpet students require instruction in:

1. The manner in which the instrument works;
2. The parts of the instrument;
3. Proper maintenance procedures (daily, weekly, and monthly activities);
4. Correct sitting and standing posture;
5. Proper hand position and finger angles;
6. How to discern and replicate a basic pulse;
7. How to consistently produce the instrument's characteristic sound;
8. How to read music (notes and rhythms);
9. How to translate written notes into specific pitches;
10. How to interpret written notation (expression, dynamics, tempo, timbre);
11. How to disassemble and reassemble the instrument; and
12. Basic breathing techniques and embouchure development.

Of course, mastery of item 10 implies a somewhat higher level of musical sophistication on the part of the student. But other than the last two items, this list represents areas of fundamental instruction applicable to *all* beginning instrumentalists, whether they've enrolled in band, orchestra, or mariachi class. Increasing specificity in the areas of technical and stylistic development will naturally occur as the students progress.

Trumpet students who are taught the keys, scales, and characteristic articulations of both band and mariachi music are certainly the better for it—and, ultimately, so are both the band and mariachi ensembles. As these students mature musically and intellectually, they become increasingly able to perceive the inherent stylistic differences between the characteristic band and mariachi sounds. It is the responsibility of the band and mariachi instructors to provide appropriate listening opportunities—in both recorded and live concert contexts—so our students will internalize these stylistic differences and then apply them appropriately in performance. In this manner, they become students of their instrument and not simply of a specific repertoire.

One need only listen to the members of Mariachi Cobre performing with a symphony orchestra or those of Mariachi Sol de México performing a tribute to Glenn Miller, the Beach Boys, or Stevie Wonder to comprehend that our students are not living in a world of musical exclusivity or some sort of cultural vacuum. (Check their iPods or CD collections!) Their daily experience is that of a multicultural society in which love for and performance of multiple forms, genres, and styles of music is a highly desirable goal. As teachers, we ought to minimize our students' exposure to and participation in our own professional jealousies and musical sectarianism. Our goal should be to produce musicians whose training prepares them for future exploration of *all types of music*—from classical to contemporary and country western, from jazz to mariachi and marching band—*wherever* their future tastes and sensibilities might guide them. We should focus on opening up opportunities rather than shutting them down.

This chapter, then, addresses itself to those mariachi programs in which the trumpet students—for whatever reason—are not concurrently enrolled in the band program and, thus, look to the mariachi teacher as the sole source of their trumpet instruction. We begin by addressing some of the basic issues involved in the teaching of trumpet fundamentals and progress toward the discussion of more advanced topics, such as specific articulations relevant to the performance of the standard mariachi repertoire. We conclude with the presentation of a number of practice suggestions and exercises that are designed to help develop our trumpet students' technical abilities in both the individual and mariachi ensemble settings.

It is the opinion of the members of the MENC National Mariachi Advisory Committee that, whenever possible, instruction of beginning mariachi students should be delivered in instrumentally homogeneous classes. That is, students may be grouped into "Beginner Trumpet Class" and "Intermediate Violin Class" rather than "Beginner Mariachi Class," "Intermediate Mariachi Class," and so forth. At the developmental level, integration of the trumpet players into a mariachi ensemble alongside the violinists and *armonías* players may best be accomplished in before- and after-school ensemble rehearsals once the students have reached a reasonable level of instrumental proficiency.

In this manner, each young musician in each of the ensemble's sections is allowed to develop his or her level of musical competence at a pedagogically appropriate rate, not according to the dictates of an ensemble's needs. For example, while performing an ensemble piece in concert D or A major may be relatively easy for inexperienced violinists and guitarists, mastering the notes of the corresponding scales required for trumpeters to participate in that ensemble is pedagogically unrealistic and inappropriate. These trumpet players are just not ready—yet. Attendees of mariachi conferences throughout the United States and Mexico will also have witnessed a similar predilection for presenting individual workshop classes in homogeneous groupings—"Beginner *Guitarrón* Class," "Intermediate Violin II Class," and so forth—except at the highest or "masters" levels.

INSTRUMENT ACQUISITION

During the first month of class, beginner trumpet players should be given a syllabus describing the kinds of things they will learn during the course of the year. This can be especially effective if the teacher performs the scales and some of the songs that the students can look forward to learning, indicating the month by which they can expect to have mastered them. At the same time, students may be given daily grades for turning in the paperwork necessary for participation in the mariachi program, such as field trip permission forms, media release forms, and, if the student's parents have decided to rent a trumpet from the school district, the instrument use form. Students also need to bring in money for a uniform dry cleaning deposit and for the purchase of whichever method book has been adopted by the mariachi trumpet instructor.

It is rarely a good idea to encourage parents of beginners to acquire instruments on their own because they too often end up with unsuitable ones, as explained in chapter 1.

Most families decide to either enroll in the school district's in-house instrument rental program or—especially with more advanced students—to exercise the option to engage in a rent-to-own arrangement with a local dealer. To the latter end, the director should invite several local musical instrument dealers to the school for a formalized "mariachi instrument drive." Soliciting the participation of multiple music stores is important in order to avoid alienating any of the individual local dealers. Cultivating good, working relationships with these key members of the local music community can prove advantageous over time.

Informational letters in both English and Spanish (or the language spoken in the home) should be sent home with the students well in advance of the event. This activity can be coordinated with the violin and guitar students into one big "instrument night" or held separately to provide a more intimate, informational setting in which to invite and address individual parent questions and concerns. Dealers can also discuss the desirability of purchasing instrument insurance. In cooperation with both parents and the instrument providers, a deadline for instrument acquisition should be clearly established. This will help ensure that, when the teacher decides to begin actual instruction on the trumpet, every student in the class has an acceptable horn in his or her lap.

PARTS AND CARE OF THE TRUMPET

Young instrumentalists need to be able to converse intelligently about making music with their instruments, and learning the names of the various parts is a logical place to start. Having the students make a drawing of the trumpet—including all the valves, slides, and keys—can be an enjoyable activity for the students, as well as a good icebreaker during the first week of school. Proceeding from the mouthpiece to the bell, the names of various parts of the trumpet can be identified and discussed. If, as is often the case, the students speak at least some Spanish, this exercise can be performed bilingually. Good, professional-quality diagrams of trumpets are available in virtually any beginner method book the teacher may choose to adopt as the classroom text. These might include:

- *Premier Performance: An Innovative and Comprehensive Band Method,* by Ed Sueta. Ed Sueta Music Publications, 1999.
- *Essential Elements: A Comprehensive Band Method,* by Tom C. Rhodes, Donald Bierschenk, Tim Lautzenheiser, and John Higgins. Hal Leonard, 1991.
- *First Division Band Method,* by Fred Weber. First Division Publishing Corporation, 1962.
- *Standard of Excellence: Comprehensive Band Method,* by Bruce Pearson. Kjos Music Company, 1996.

For the next week or so, a portion of each class period may be spent drawing a trumpet on the chalkboard following specific instructions from the students as to the location, size, and function of the various parts. You may also hold up an actual trumpet and have individual students name each part as you point to it. Once the students are able to name and label all the parts on a written test, it is time for them to disassemble the trumpet, part by part, following your instructions. Before reassembling, demonstrate the use of specially made brushes for cleaning mouthpieces and valve casings, a lead-pipe cleaning "snake," and valve oil and slide grease. Consistently emphasize the importance of overall cleanliness. Once the trumpet has been reassembled, you can test for student success by having them try to produce a tone, for unless all valves and slides have been reassembled correctly, no sound can be produced.

As with any musical instrument, trumpets should not be left unattended in places, such as the schoolyard, cafeteria, gym, back porch, or the houses of friends and relatives. Each student should be assigned designated cabinet space in the mariachi room to store his or her instrument during the course of the school day. At home it should be kept out of the hands of younger siblings or friends. Students should also be informed of the dangers of leaving instruments exposed to extreme temperatures, such as in the trunk of the car in hot weather.

MUSIC LITERACY

As the thoroughness of students' preparation in the area of music literacy is often quite varied, a safe strategy is to presume no prior knowledge on the part of students and to begin by introducing note names, lines and spaces, note values, and so forth. The adopted trumpet method book will present this in a sequential fashion, leading up to performance on the instrument.

As the deadline for trumpet acquisition approaches, the teacher can alternate teaching the fundamentals of musical literacy with the teaching and testing of trumpet part names and maintenance procedures. When teaching young beginners, this practice of varying the instructional activities has the added benefit of appreciably lengthening students' attention span. Then, when the deadline arrives, the entire class can hit the ground running, making the connection between theory and practice.

SITTING POSTURE AND BREATHING TECHNIQUE

Show students proper performance posture by having them study illustrations in the method book and compare these pictures with observation of the teacher. Demonstrate your own personal performance posture—standing and sitting, both with and without a trumpet—for the students to imitate. Explain the importance of maintaining a gentle curvature of the right-hand fingers and wrist to avoid possible injuries, such as carpal tunnel syndrome. Emphasize that all these techniques are to be mastered before performance on actual instruments begins. This tends to make the students work extra hard to perform these exercises conscientiously.

Numerous exercises are available to help develop proper breathing practices. Hissing exercises are beneficial for improving long-tone production. Without the use of the trumpet, students simply imitate the hissing sound of a snake for a specified number of beats (see figure 8.1). Students are instructed to pay careful attention to the steady intensity

Hissing Exercises

FIGURE 8.1

and speed of the airstream produced. They can begin with whole notes, half notes, and quarter notes and then expand to include two or three tied whole notes (eight to twelve beats) in the exercises. These fundamental exercises should be performed with great care and precision, as the inculcation of proper breathing techniques is prerequisite to the production of a good, solid trumpet tone.

EMBOUCHURE

One way to illustrate proper embouchure is to have the students blow through a straw. The lips will be forced to tighten on the sides while leaving an aperture in the center to allow air to pass through. Later, students can be given pieces of paper upon which to practice buzzing techniques. The only way they can make the paper buzz is through tightening the corners of their lips.

When the students are able to consistently produce a strong buzzing sound, it is time to place the mouthpiece on the lips. The instructor should explain precisely how to place the mouthpiece onto the lips. A common error against which students should be cautioned is pressing the mouthpiece too tightly against the lips. Common axioms recommend either positioning the mouthpiece evenly over the upper and lower lips or allocating one third of the mouthpiece to the upper lip and two thirds to the lower lip. Steve Carrillo, lead trumpeter for Mariachi Cobre, on the other hand, puts two thirds of the mouthpiece over the upper lip and one third over the lower lip. Thus, we must acknowledge that there is no "one-size-fits-all" formula at work here. What is important is finding a comfortable individual embouchure that will allow each student to be successful. Remember, each person is physically unique, and the ultimate goal is a beautiful tone.

Students can become comfortable with the production of the buzzing sound by performing the hissing exercises while buzzing on the mouthpiece. Proficiency, however, may be acquired only after a few weeks of daily practice, but once this step is mastered, it is time to place the mouthpiece into the trumpet itself. We recommended that students begin with a 7C mouthpiece size, as its characteristic shape is amenable to most beginners. As skill levels develop, however, aperture size and cup depth become a matter of personal preference and comfort. Again, since each student's mouth and teeth are inherently different, experimentation with various mouthpieces is recommended before any final decisions are made.

When students begin performing on the assembled trumpet, the immediate goal is the consistent production of a good, solid, characteristic tone. This might best be achieved through the performance of long-tone exercises, beginning on middle C. Students should begin with whole notes, breathing through the nose or the corners of the mouth—without actually removing the mouthpiece from the lips. After they are consistently able to produce a good sound on this note, they may proceed up a full step to D. Instruct the students to pull out the third valve slide about a half inch to ensure good intonation. This process should continue up the C major scale, until the students reach G on the second line of the staff, and downward to the A below middle C. When most members of the class are able to demonstrate a consistently good tone on all these notes, it is time to move more systematically into the method book.

METHOD BOOKS AND ESTABLISHING A DAILY ROUTINE

There are many method books on the market. Some tend to introduce material too quickly; others omit items you might personally consider essential. While any method book offers the benefit of providing overall structure to the teaching of the instrument, the conscientious instructor should be open to incorporating additional exercises that complement the method book. As you gain experience as a trumpet teacher, you will discover that no single method book—or trumpet clinician—approaches all pedagogical issues more successfully than all others. By becoming familiar with and mixing and matching these different approaches, you will eventually be able to assemble your own teaching methodology, incorporating the best ideas encountered from a variety of sources.

By around the tenth or twelfth week of school, a daily routine will have been established. This routine should be used through December and ought to include the following:

- Breathing exercises,
- Buzzing exercises without mouthpiece,
- Buzzing exercises with mouthpiece,
- Long tones with trumpet,
- A daily warm-up that gradually ascends the scale,
- Vocal exercises,
- Method book exercises, and
- Mariachi repertoire.

In order to perform their first few pieces with the rest of the mariachi ensemble, trumpet students will need to be comfortable playing in keys with three or even four sharps. One method that may be used in teaching the concepts of sharps and naturals is to introduce a middle C$\sharp$ as a variant of the open middle C natural that they already know. Both notes appear on the first line below the staff, so students must be told that whenever they see a sharp before middle C, a different fingering is required. They must use a "1-2-3" fingering, depressing all three valves with the third valve slide pulled out rather than leaving them all open.

A more formal explanation of key signatures leads the students to understand that each individual signature tells them which notes to play sharp and which ones to play natural. Introduction of the F$\sharp$, G$\sharp$, and D$\sharp$ follows. Although the first ensemble song will probably have three or four sharps, if your students practice these notes every day, they will understand the concept and have no problem playing them in the concert.

Take special care in selecting the mariachi repertoire for the December winter concert. Here are some areas of consideration:

- Range,
- Rhythmic features,
- Part playing, and
- Cultural sensitivity.

There should be a range of about a fifth, and include mostly long tones. Make sure each piece includes places to rest since beginner trumpet players tend to tire easily. Beginner students should perform in unison, as the standard mariachi practice of performing in harmony will not be introduced until the second semester.

It is recommended that directors obtain a catalogue of mariachi sheet music and acquire literature appropriate for beginning trumpet players. The director may also choose to make arrangements of non-traditional mariachi pieces, such as "Jingle Bells" and "Away in a Manger," for performance in the winter concert. Like all music teachers, however, it is imperative that the mariachi instructor remain highly sensitive to the students' religious beliefs, specifically on the topic of what is acceptable and appropriate Christmas repertoire, as they come from all points throughout our increasingly multicultural, multireligious (and nonreligious) society.

Once this first concert is over, it is time to expand the technical abilities of the students. Lip slurs should be introduced, along with scales in sharp keys in range order:

- Concert G major (A major scale for trumpets—lower octave)
- Concert A major (B major scale for trumpets)
- Concert B♭ major (C major scale for trumpets)
- Concert C major (D major scale for trumpets)
- Concert D major (E major scale for trumpets)
- Concert E major (F♯ major scale for trumpets)
- Concert F major (G major scale for trumpets)

See figure 8.13 for trumpet scale exercises.

Nothing is deleted from the warm-up routine; rather, it is expanded. Trumpet players must develop the discipline to practice on an everyday basis, as "lip memory" is crucial when learning new notes and new exercises.

The Beginner Trumpet Etudes presented in figure 8.2 are a good example of a beginner warm-up. Special care has been taken in introduc-

Beginner Trumpet Etudes

Noé Sánchez
©2004

FIGURE 8.2

ing students to long-tone production. Learning to differentiate between the various note values is also incorporated into the warm-up, as is range expansion. Steady work in the method book will ensure that students are learning new musical terms and beginning to recognize and perform more difficult rhythm patterns. The relationships between the skills developed in the exercises and warm-ups—such as note values, lip position, stamina, and embouchure—and the musical requirements of the repertoire introduced should be made explicit by the director, helping the students make a direct connection between their daily routine and the repertoire they are learning.

PRACTICING

We often forget to teach students precisely how to practice. Although the concept is seemingly easily understood by adults, many youngsters take their instruments home without really knowing how to go about practicing. Many develop the habit of pulling their instruments out of their cases and going straight to their repertoire. A productive home practice session should include a specific routine by which the student can warm up effectively, review and reinforce known skills, work on improving technique, develop new skills, and apply these skills to the performance of specific repertoire. These factors are codified in figures 8.1 and 8.2.

"HOW TO PRACTICE AT HOME"

Follow the daily trumpet practice routine (see tables 8.1 and 8.2), and keep the following things in mind:

- Hold the trumpet properly.
- Sit or stand up straight while practicing.
- Concentrate on using correct embouchure.
- Buy and use your own music stand.
- Buy and use your own metronome.
- Practice in front of a mirror to observe correct posture and embouchure.

- Record yourself once a week, and critique your performance.
- Practice *every* day.
- Practice with a purpose; more will be achieved in less time.

To this end, we have included at the end of this chapter a section titled "Practice Procedure" that will help reinforce what the instructor is teaching in the class setting at school.

Since the teacher will not be present, students should practice in front of a mirror so that they can make adjustments and correct themselves. Provide students with mutes if family members complain that the trumpet is too loud. Unless it is absolutely necessary, however, try to avoid this practice, as it will not help your beginners produce the solid characteristic tone desired at this stage. Insist that your students warm up properly every time they play, and emphasize prac-

Table 8.1.   Warm-Up/Practice Routine (Beginners)

1. Buzzing/Long Tones/Low Notes	5 minutes
2. Beginner Etudes or Warm-Up (play slowly, do not "blast," start with low notes)	5 minutes
3. Rest	1 minute
4. Scales (play each note in tune, without forcing)	5 minutes
5. *Círculos*	5 minutes
6. Rest	1 minute
7. Repertoire (practice measure by measure, slowly)	10 minutes
Total:	32 minutes

Table 8.2.   Warm-Up/Practice Routine (Intermediate/Advanced)

1. Buzzing/Long Tones/Low Notes	5 minutes
2. Rest	1 minute
3. Lip Slurs	5 minutes
4. Rest	1 minute
5. Scales (play each note in tune, without forcing)	10 minutes
6. Rest	1 minute
7. Lip Slurs, *Círculos*, Vibrato	10 minutes
8. Rest	1 minute
9. Double- and Triple-Tonguing (advanced students)	5 minutes
10. Rest	1 minute
11. Repertoire (practice measure by measure, slowly)	20 minutes
Total:	60 minutes

ticing softly. When it comes to trumpet, one doesn't play the way one practices.

As indicated in this routine, beginner trumpet players need to take short breaks between exercises. It is not beneficial to continue playing with fatigued lips, as this may result in physical damage. Many middle school students wear braces on their teeth. They should have no real problems playing the trumpet, but they may wish to protect their lips with a wax or plastic mouth guard, usually available from their orthodontist. Warn all students against using the right pinkie finger to apply excessive pressure with the mouthpiece against the lips; they should concentrate on tightening the corners of the lips. (Note: The right-hand pinkie finger should remain relaxed, resting gently on top of the "hook" or "finger ring" located on the lead pipe. It should not be inserted into the ring itself, as this will greatly diminish the mobility of the ring finger due to the unique biological arrangement of the tendons in the hand.)

Mariachi trumpet students find themselves in an educationally advantageous situation. They will learn fundamentals from a band method book, which will—at least initially—tend to focus on performing in flat keys. They will simultaneously be introduced by their mariachi teacher to the sharp keys typically favored by the mariachi's historic instrumentation, which features violins and the indigenous or folk instruments— the *vihuela*, guitar, *guitarra de golpe*, and *guitarrón*. As mentioned earlier, students should follow a progression of keys from low to high: concert G, A, B♭, C, D, E, and F major.

By the second semester, the students' ranges will improve as the instructor demonstrates the proper technique for reaching the higher notes. After performing a proper warm-up, this would include:

- Maintaining solid breath support,
- Producing a faster airstream,
- Tightening of the corners of the lips, and
- Going from a *tu* to a *tee* vowel sound inside the mouth.

Students are encouraged to become comfortable with the fact that improvement on the trumpet is gradual at the beginning. They must faithfully adhere to their daily routine and persevere in the method book. Ensure that the level of the ensemble repertoire matches that of the method book lessons and the technical abilities of the students. Therefore, if a mariachi arrangement is purchased, the range and rhythms should be carefully considered.

TEACHING MARIACHI TRUMPET STYLE

Although there is no single way of teaching mariachi style to beginner students, critically listening to recordings is essential. When it comes to trumpet, the most influential mariachi performer is Miguel Martínez. He is widely credited with single-handedly creating the mariachi trumpet style. Students will derive great benefit from listening to his performances on Mariachi Vargas de Tecalitlán recordings from the 1950s, 1960s, 1970s, and early 1980s, which illustrate his style in great depth and breadth. His influence is also evident in the more contemporary recordings of both the Mariachi Vargas and other leading mariachis, such as Mariachi Sol de México, Mariachi Los Camperos de Nati Cano, Mariachi Cobre, Mariachi México de Pepe Villa, and Mariachi América de Jesús Rodríguez de Híjar.

Young trumpet players should try to internalize and imitate the sound and style of these recordings. Critical listening will also make standard mariachi articulations and tonguings more accessible. Students can also try to make connections with the violin bowings and the strumming patterns (*mánicos*) of the *armonías* sections, as these articulations often mirror those of the trumpets. Whenever possible, observe the rhythms of ballet *folklórico* dancers, as they, too, reflect many of the articulations of the guitars, thus providing the trumpets with a guide.

VIBRATO

The recommended way of acquiring and adapting a traditional mariachi trumpet vibrato is to develop a jaw vibrato. Use a metronome to create

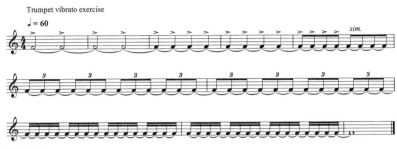

FIGURE 8.3

a process by which the student subdivides the beat into increasingly smaller parts. Steve Carrillo of Mariachi Cobre recalls being taught to perform the characteristic mariachi vibrato many years ago by one of today's greatest mariachi trumpet players, Federico Torres, of the Mariachi Vargas de Tecalitlán. Instruct your students to perform the following exercise regularly, repeating as needed (see figure 8.3).

Play the first note normally. When the next note is introduced, drop the jaw slightly. Repeat this process throughout the exercise. Use a metronome to clearly reinforce the rhythmic subdivisions. When this exercise is mastered, trumpets will be able to oscillate in time; the individual students' vibratos will match because they are replicating the exact subdivisions. Make sure the vibrato is controlled, not spread or wide.

TONGUING

Articulation patterns—tonguing, in particular—are rarely written in mariachi sheet music by arrangers. Understanding of what constitutes accepted "mariachi style" is often simply assumed, so it is up to the mariachi instructor to provide guidance as to how to articulate in a stylistically appropriate manner. Besides its characteristic vibrato, mariachi trumpet articulation is slightly different from that cultivated in band music. One such important difference in mariachi style is the way the staccatos are produced. When a staccato is performed in band music, it is usually achieved by producing a short *tu* sound. In mariachi music,

FIGURE 8.4

FIGURE 8.5

however, the staccato is actually closed at the end, so a *tut* articulation is performed. Figure 8.4 is an example to help clarify.

Since it is difficult to know precisely when to employ particular articulation patterns, several examples of popular mariachi music are provided in this chapter. Note, however, that these are merely suggestions. As noted earlier, both students and teachers should develop the habit of regularly listening to mariachi recordings to begin internalizing and imitating the style. Regular attendance at mariachi conferences will help both teachers and students learn to articulate in a recognizably "mariachi fashion." All the examples that follow are written in concert keys, so the trumpet parts are already transposed.

The "Mariachi Círculos Warm-Ups" are provided in figure 8.14. These exercises were originally created to teach and drill the typical *armonías* chord progressions. Thus, while the *armonías* are practicing specific chord changes, the trumpets (and violins) may simultaneously cultivate the typical *bolero* sound (see figure 8.5).

"Las Mañanitas," the ubiquitous birthday song and Mothers' Day serenade, is one of the most frequently performed pieces within the mariachi repertoire. The instrumental introduction and middle transition section of the song are presented here. Notice the total absence of slurs in figure 8.6. The typical endings of *rancheras* in 3/4 time may be given various interpretations. Figure 8.7 is an example of one way to articulate this very common ending formula.

The polka and the closely related *ranchera "polqueada"* are two genres integral to the mariachi repertoire. Observe in figure 8.8 the example of a typical articulation pattern presented in "Atotonilco," composed by Dr. Juan José Espinosa. Mariachis play a variety of musical genres, a number of which require the production of a lyrical timbre. Sebastián Yradier's world-famous "La Paloma" demonstrates the *danza habanera* genre with its distinctive lyrical sound (see figure 8.9).

The style that demonstrates a totally unique mariachi sound is the *son jalisciense*. Three well-known examples of this genre, "Camino Real de Colima," "El Relámpago," and "La Negra," have been presented in figures 8.10 and 8.11. Notice all articulations; they are not what nonmariachi trumpet players would have typically chosen to play. Proper articulation of the traditional ending patterns for the *son jalisciense* is another often neglected but stylistically critical aspect of trumpet playing. In figure 8.12, we demonstrate two of the most common.

Las Mañanitas

FIGURE 8.6

Ranchera ending in 3/4

FIGURE 8.7

Atotonilco

FIGURE 8.8

La Paloma

FIGURE 8.9

FIGURE 8.10

FIGURE 8.11

FIGURE 8.12

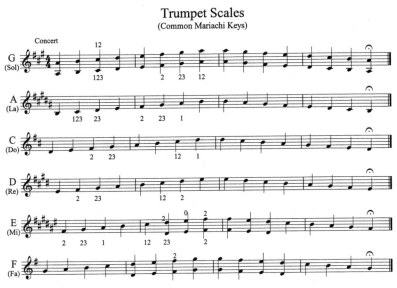

FIGURE 8.13

CONCLUSION

In summary, the curriculum of instruction for mariachi trumpet players should be directed toward the sequential development of a solid technical foundation. It is of utmost importance that trumpet players consistently practice a warm-up sequence such as that shown in the "How to Practice at Home" section. Using a standard method book is highly recommended as well. Choose repertoire suitable for young trumpet players' range and rhythm patterns.

If a published arrangement seems perfectly suited to the other instruments of the mariachi ensemble but is not pedagogically appropriate for your trumpeters, take the time to rearrange the trumpet parts to match the specific needs of your students. Temporarily transposing the higher trumpet part down an octave may be the only adjustment necessary. Make the various tonguing and vibrato exercises presented here available to your students, and encourage them to try to incorporate them in their daily performance. Finally, make a habit with your students of critically listening to recordings of leading mariachi trumpet players, as this is absolutely essential to the development of an appreciation for and understanding of the unique style used in the characteristic interpretation of traditional mariachi repertoire.

FROM: GRADANTE " ¡ECHENLE CON GANAS, MUCHACHOS!" (PAGE 3—ALL VOLUMES) PRACTICE PROCEDURE

When preparing to practice—especially when beginning a new piece—please observe the following guidelines:

1. *Time Signature:* Check the Time Signature to discover how many beats there are in each measure and what kind of note receives one beat.
2. *Key Signature:* Check the Key Signature to identify the key of the selection and discover whether the selection features any key changes. Review appropriate scales, arpeggios, and/or chord progressions.
3. *Accidentals:* Check the selection for any accidentals (sharps, flats, or naturals placed beside individual notes). Check the fingerings for any

such notes and try to determine whether these notes indicate a key change.

4. *Endings/Coda Phrases:* Scan the selection for any Endings or Coda Phrases:

1st Ending	*D.C. al Fine*	*D.C. al Coda*	*Fine*	*To Coda*
2nd Ending	*D.S. al Fine*	*D.S. al Coda*	*Coda*	*Segno*

5. *New Materials:* Identify any new or difficult rhythms, notes, performance techniques, or chords. Learn or review these before trying to play the entire selection.

6. *Mindset:* Adopt a mental attitude or mindset that is appropriate for the style or genre of music you are about to perform. We are aware of the differences between *boleros, rancheras, boleros rancheros, huapangos, pasodobles, polkas, cumbias, jarabes, joropos, danzas, danzones,* and *sones*—as well as classical, rock, jazz, hip hop, or country music—to name just a few examples. Thus, we should not set about to perform all of them in the same manner. Music has emotion—let's learn to express it appropriately.

7. *Reflect & Review:* Identify any passages that appear repeatedly throughout the music. Try to detect possible trouble spots in the selection. Isolate, review, or re-learn these passages. Avoid making the same mistakes that were made in the last practice session. Have specific goals in mind. Ask yourself: "Exactly what do I want to accomplish in this practice session? How will learning this passage help get me closer to finishing the entire piece?"

8. *Ending Practice:* Wipe your instrument clean, put it carefully into its case, and return it to the cabinet. Pick up and safely store all of your materials.

Don't leave your things on the floor, under your chair, or on your stand!

Trumpets

Mariachi Círculos Warmups

Noé Sánchez
©2002

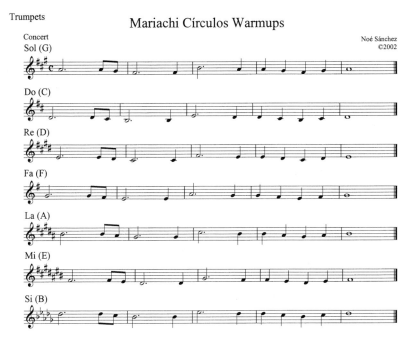

FIGURE 8.14

9

Teaching the Mariachi Harp*

SERGIO "CHECO" ALONSO

Throughout the twentieth century, mariachi experienced a transformation at the expense of what was arguably the tradition's most important instrument: *el arpa jalisciense* (harp from Jalisco). During the mariachi's process of urbanization, popularization, and commercialization, the *arpa jalisciense* or *arpa de mariachi* (mariachi harp) greatly diminished in importance within the ensemble to the point where it disappeared almost entirely among the popular urban groups that emerged.

Today, the harp appears to be making a comeback among Mexican and Mexican American mariachi musicians throughout the southwestern United States. Finding inspiration in the mariachi traditions of the past, young musicians are now attempting to integrate the harp into their ensembles. Though this endeavor often proves difficult due to limited availability of harp instruction, it is well worth the effort: the harp is a versatile, colorful instrument with a longstanding tradition in Mexico and mariachi.

---

*Parts of this article are based on information available online at www.mariachieducationresources.com. Used with permission.

HARP STUDY IN MARIACHI MUSIC PROGRAMS

High-quality harp study in school mariachi programs is central to the instrument's survival. Unlike other mariachi instruments, very few instructional resources are available for harp. Lack of teachers; method books; sheet music; and a well-established, definitive mode of performance are the greatest challenges facing potential harp students. In addition, there is not likely to be a "harp class" at the present time due to budget concerns and limited interest. Music teachers can address these needs and aid in the instrument's dissemination by acquiring basic knowledge of the harp, developing pedagogy for its instruction, and then nurturing their students' interest. Institutionalized and codified harp study, then, is critical to the revitalization, reinvention, and reaffirmation of its place in the mariachi.

Redefining the harp's role must also be a task for the entire mariachi community; harpists must develop the necessary skills for its successful performance, while composers, arrangers, and directors must integrate the harp in new and exciting ways into musical arrangements. Most important, the mariachi culture itself must place greater demands on the instrument and have higher expectations of its practitioners.

AN APPROACH TO HARP STUDY

The mariachi's most versatile instrument is currently played with the least versatility. Often playing "second fiddle" to the rest of the ensemble, the harp has not enjoyed the level of technical development of the other mariachi instruments or that of other Latin American harp traditions. So much has it dwindled in importance within the genre that it has come to be regarded as an unnecessary component to the standard ensemble, too often integrated for the sake of visual aesthetic and serving as an "ornament" for groups wanting to emulate the traditional look of the rural mariachi.

A sound approach to the study of mariachi harp must begin with the focus, discipline, perseverance, care, and passion it demands, as with all mariachi instruments. Lack of information about the harp has hindered its role within the contemporary mariachi tradition: novice harpists do not have the appropriate guidance and/or resources and have fallen short in their attempts to understand its many complexities. No other instrument in the ensemble offers such a variety of techniques and performance effects as well as wealth of musical color. Therefore, it is the responsibility of harp students to make honest efforts to study, develop, and apply the many facets of harp performance.

As a teacher, you have an important role to play. Emphasize dedication and commitment to the fundamentals of precise playing technique. First and foremost, concentrate on studying the most common techniques and genres of the traditional mariachi, particularly the *son jalisciense* and the *ranchera*. Then, encourage students to explore the many possibilities when playing other genres. Because today's mariachi plays such a wide variety of music, it is important that students acquire and execute techniques that are common to other Mexican and Latin American harp traditions. There are countless ways to integrate new technical devices into mariachi without sacrificing the integrity of the music.

Included here are exercises and suggestions to help you get your students on the right harp-playing path. First, a few things to consider:

1. Individual study. Assuming that you will not have a classroom full of harpists, this material is geared toward a small group or individual study. I invite you to use pedagogy that you are most comfortable with to introduce these concepts to your harp student(s).

2. Right hand, left hand, both hands! While harp performance typically reserves specific techniques for each hand, here we develop both hands with the same degree of efficiency. As a given, practice one hand first, then the other, and finally both hands together.

3. Music theory. Complement harp study with music theory. It is essential that your students have a firm understanding of major and minor scales as well as basic harmony.

4. The key of C major. Tune your instrument to C major, as all exercises will be in this key. Your students may later apply these concepts to any

key as they become more proficient in basic musicianship and harp technique.

STRUCTURAL CHARACTERISTICS

There is no absolute standard in the construction of folk harps of western Mexico. Regional, local, and even individual preferences among harp makers allow for slight variations in size, shape, and materials. Nonetheless, several features distinguish mariachi harps from other types of Latin American folk harps, the two most important being that they are centrally located in the state of Jalisco and that they were integral components of the mariachi ensembles. It is because of these commonalties that they are collectively known as *Jalisco* or mariachi harps.

The mariachi harp is a thirty-six-string diatonic instrument, constructed primarily of cedar, ash, mahogany, and *tacote* (a balsa-like wood native to western Mexico used in constructing the soundboard only). The sound box consists of seven completely closed panels: five are joined to make up the very large "belly," and two are fused to make the "barn door" base and legs. The *tacote* soundboard typically exhibits a lengthwise grain with four sound holes of decreasing diameter running up the length of the harp, two on each side of the string plane. The general shape of the sound box is deep and wide at the base and narrower toward the top.

The neck of the mariachi harp has a very gentle curvature, almost appearing to be a straight bar, and is sometimes decorated with a cockscomb on the top side. While the tuning pegs were once primarily made of wood, it is common today to find aluminum or steel pegs. One of the more interesting details of the mariachi harp is that it has no bridge pins; the knotted strings run directly from the soundboard up the left side of the neck and into the tuning pegs. The knots hold the strings in place in the soundboard. Although gut strings were formerly used, nylon strings are more common today.

A recent adaptation to the harp is retractable feet, which make the harp easier to transport. Another recent adaptation is the use of tuning levers. While levers are not traditional on a Jalisco harp, they allow the modern mariachi harpist to modulate and perform chromatic harmonies quickly and easily. Levers may be integrated on all of the strings or only some of the strings.

CARING FOR YOUR HARP

Like any wooden musical instrument, the harp's worst enemies are heat and low humidity. Store your harp at room temperature, and avoid exposing it to abrupt changes in climate. During performances, try to keep it away from direct sunlight. Never leave it in an automobile for an extended period of time, especially during extreme temperatures, as heat cracks the wood and softens the glue. Keep it in a safe location where human traffic is minimal to avoid accidentally tipping it over. Put it in a position where nothing will fall on it. Always store it horizontally, and never leave it leaning against a wall. Store it in a soft case to protect it from bruises and dust.

Wipe the harp daily with a dry cloth to remove dust. For settled and penetrated dust, you may use a damp, but never wet, cloth. You may also use wood polish for musical instruments to wipe away hand oils. Have your students always keep their hands clean. Mariachis may play in the roughest of terrains, so during a gig, instruct your students to avoid setting up in dirty, wet, or rough areas. Slightly loosen the strings when transporting the harp long distances, especially on an airplane.

CHANGING STRINGS

Changing strings can be difficult, but with practice and experience, it becomes much easier. As you begin, remember that strings are specifically designed for each harp. Features such as material, length, and diameter are critical in establishing the correct tension of each string. To prevent damage, make sure that the particular strings you use are the correct ones for your instrument. In general, the treble and midrange strings range from about .025 to .055 gauge, and the bass strings are wrapped in nylon with either a nylon or fiber core.

At the Soundboard

- Bass Strings: Reach inside the harp through the largest sound hole and insert the string through the appropriate string hole from the inside out. Pull up on the string until the pad touches the inside of the soundboard.

- Midrange Strings: Insert the string down through the string hole and continue pushing until you can reach that end from the largest sound hole. Make a bundle of about three knots at the bottom end, clip off excess string, and then pull up on the string until the knots touch the inside of the soundboard.

- Treble Strings: There are various ways to change treble-range strings. Here is my preferred method:
    1. Make two loops at one end of the string and put the smaller one through the larger.
    2. With the smaller loop protruding through the larger, pull on both ends of the string to tighten the knot.
    3. When the knot is nearly closed, insert a thicker string or finishing nail through the knot and continue tightening.
    4. Tighten the knot and clip off the excess string.
    5. Insert the knot vertically down the string hole. On some harps, reinsert the string peg.

At the Neck

1. Fish the string through the eye from the bottom up, and then turn the peg clockwise.
2. Position the string end so that it pinches itself after a half turn.
3. Guide the string toward the inside as you continue to turn.
4. You should reach the appropriate pitch at about three complete turns. Clip off excess string.

TUNING

The harp is traditionally tuned diatonically in the key of G or C, where the lowest string is G1 (an eighteenth below middle C) and the highest is G6 (a nineteenth above middle C). However, due to the complexities of contemporary arrangements, harpists today tune in a variety of different keys. Whatever the key, the strings are always tuned to the same pitch name and simply sharped or flatted as needed.

For lever harps, I recommend tuning in B♭, as it allows you quick and easy access to the most common keys that mariachi music is played today: B♭, F, C, G, D, A, E, and their relative minors. When performing songs in minor keys, it is best to tune in either melodic minor or harmonic minor (to allow for the dominant seventh chord).

An electronic chromatic tuner is a great investment for any harpist. Boss TU Series Chromatic Tuners seem to be the devices of choice for many harpists, as they have a wide tuning range suitable for the harp.

PLAYING POSITION

No two students are built the same. Therefore, you will always find slight variations in harp placement and body positioning. Nevertheless, there are numerous things to consider when developing your students' playing position that take into account their well-being. A correct playing position is one that always minimizes the potential for injury and promotes good health.

Legs, Torso, and Neck

A good posture begins at the foundation. Feet should be placed shoulder-width apart with legs slightly bent at the knees. While I tend to stand with my left leg a bit forward, many harpists position their feet side by side. Either way, your students must stand tall, balanced, and completely relaxed. Have them avoid leaning on either leg or locking at the knees. The torso must also remain lined up with the neck and head directly in balance, ensuring that students do not slouch or tilt their heads either way. Maintaining a comfortable and relaxed standing position relieves stress in the lower back and neck and minimizes the risk of strain and injury.

The harp should stand directly in front of the body and lean toward the body so that the top comes to rest on the right shoulder. In the case where the harp is too short (or your students are too tall) and it does not reach the shoulder, it should be placed on the right side of the chest. Never place it under the right arm, as this hinders blood circulation and limits mobility.

Arms, Elbows, and Shoulders

Correct arm position depends on the proper placement and movement of the elbows and shoulders. Shoulders should always remain down and relaxed; elbows must face down, with forearms parallel to the floor while leading arm movement. The arms themselves should be nearly symmetric, with the right forearm remaining horizontal and the left slightly slanted upward. With respect to proper shifting, we aim to achieve "efficiency of motion" by eliminating all unnecessary and energy-consuming movements; elbows and shoulders must freely and naturally glide the arms back and forth with the least amount of force and tension.

Wrists, Hands, and Fingers

Proper positioning of the wrists, hands, and fingers is perhaps the most critical aspect of playing position because of the tiny muscles, tendons, and ligaments that are constantly subject to strain. Incorrect form and use frequently cause injuries, such as tendonitis and carpal tunnel syndrome.

The right wrist must be positioned perpendicular to the center of the strings. Because the left arm angles down toward the strings, the left wrist is angled slightly upward. Make sure that the hands lie naturally straight without bending up or down at the wrist and that the wrists themselves do not brace on the edge of the soundboard—this will cause increased tension and strain on the tendons and ligaments. While the right palm generally faces the string plane, the left palm sometimes faces down among some harpists (e.g., *jarocho* harpists) or when executing certain passages.

The hands and fingers are placed almost level at the middle or upper part of the strings. The index, middle, and ring fingers must remain naturally curved at both joints and should be placed consistently "in line" with the thumb, where the thumb sits highest. The thumb must be kept bent backward, practically vertical. The strings must be placed at the tips of the fingers and on the outer edge of the thumb. Nails are generally left long and are filed rounded. When pulling strings, both the fingertips and the nails make contact with the strings.

During finger movement, the hands should be allowed to close naturally into a relaxed fist, where the thumb folds down on top of the other fingers. It is critical that students do not pull in a "clawlike" manner, as an open hand creates residual tension after exerting force. With respect to the thumb, the action is controlled by the lower joint, so it should always simulate a "hitchhiker's" thumb and never bend at the knuckle. Also, the pinkie, which is generally not used, must be allowed to mirror the ring finger during movement. Allowing it to fold down or stick up while playing creates an unnatural tension between it and the ring finger. Above all else, make sure to find a balance between relaxation and tension, as too much of either would be detrimental.

HARPISTIC NOTATION

While no standardized method of harp notation exists in the mariachi world, we may adopt many of the symbols used in the classical harp tradition developed by legendary harpist Carlos Salzedo.

- The Grand Staff: Notes in the treble staff are typically played with the right hand while notes in the bass staff are played with the left.
- The Numbers: Indicate the fingers that are used to play the particular note. 1 (thumb), 2 (index), 3 (middle), and 4 (ring).

- The Bracket: Indicates that all fingers under the bracket are placed simultaneously. We generally want to place the fingers in the melodic direction we are going.
- The Chord and Rolled Chord: A chord must be played flat or "unbroken." When indicated, it should be played arpeggiated from bottom to top.

Because the harp most often plays the role of bass and harmonic accompaniment, it is adequate to combine standard *guitarrón* and *armonía* notation with traditional harp notation. Standard *guitarrón* notation places all of its notes within the bass clef staff, and it is assumed (unless otherwise indicated) that the performer will execute the notated pitch and its lower octave simultaneously. Where the harp is executing bass lines and harmonic accompaniment, this notation suffices. *Armonía* instrumentalists read rhythmic notation from a treble clef staff, where chord names are notated above specific notes. Where the harp is executing bass lines and harmonic accompaniment, this notation is also adequate. Mariachi harp notation then may alternate from traditional harp notation when executing specific melodic lines (figure 9.1A) and *guitarrón* and *armonía* notation when performing only bass and harmonic accompaniment (figure 9.1B).

FIGURE 9.1

FORMS

A solid foundation for playing the harp begins with the study of chord forms. Some approaches begin instruction *melodically* by using one or two fingers, adding the third and fourth as the student becomes more proficient. I prefer to have students begin *harmonically*, with all four fingers placed simultaneously. While I am now experimenting with the pinkie finger, it is generally not used. Training students early on to view their fingers as a unit and not just as individual digits is beneficial for several reasons:

1. Harpists rely on securing positions instead of playing "one finger at a time." Unlike other string instruments that have keys or fret boards, the harp has no physical frame of reference when vibrating the strings. As a result, harpists must learn to be "in tune" with the shapes of their hands in space as their fingers are positioned in specific ways. Having your students "plan before they play" by placing fingers in the most logical preparatory positions establishes the appropriate technique for creating the best sounds. This is analogous to the classical guitarist who "plants" his or her right-hand fingers in preparation of chord arpeggiation.

2. It nurtures student musicianship skills. Students are forced to identify the chords that they are playing instead of simply executing random collections of unassociated pitches. By learning about and applying harmony as well as melody, students gain an overall understanding of music principles.

3. Students "learn to listen." Much of what harpists play is harmonic accompaniment in various keys, so students learn the appropriate pitches to play within chords as well as which pitches to avoid when playing in different keys. They condition their ears to discern how individual pitches within each chord sound with respect to each other as well as how each chord sounds relative to the tonic. This, again, is analogous to guitar playing.

Therefore, like the guitarist that trains his or her hand to grasp barred forms that may be used to execute a variety of different chords throughout the fret board, we commence with eight basic shapes:

- The basic forms consist of a triad plus the upper octave, and its two inversions.
- The triad seventh forms consist of the triad with an added seventh and its three inversions.
- The scale form is based on the series of four adjacent strings.

Form Exercises

Select any eight-string range. The range of the right hand (i.e., C3–B3) should generally be higher than the left hand (e.g., C5–B5). The ring finger should be placed on the lowest string and the thumb on the highest. For example, the root triad should be positioned as follows: string 1 (ring finger), string 3 (middle finger), string 5 (index finger), string 8 (thumb). For the sake of establishing a consistent frame of reference, I suggest placing the ring finger on a colored string.

The first exercises consist of (1) placing fingers, (2) squeezing, (3) relaxing, and (4) disengaging. Repeat this process, one hand at a time, making sure not to neglect the left hand, which for many people can be the most difficult of the two to manipulate. Your students should exert the same amount of force from each finger while maintaining a relaxed curvature. As beginners, they should be concerned with developing the proper playing position of the fingers, hands, and wrists and also familiarizing themselves with the "feel" of the form, being especially sensitive to the distance between each finger. Practice this exercise with each of the eight forms.

Building Chords and Scales

Once your students have developed a strong "feel" for the eight forms, they are ready to use them to build chords and scales. Now your students should position their forms in different locations in order to build specific chords and their respective inversions:

1. Triad-Root Position   2. Triad-1st Inversion   3. Triad-2nd Inversion

FIGURE 9.2

- Play C major three different ways (see figure 9.2):
  1. Root Position: Place the ring finger on the first note (root) of the chord in triad root form.
  2. First Inversion: Place the ring finger on the third of the chord in triad first inversion form.
  3. Second Inversion: Place the ring finger on the fifth of the chord in triad second inversion form.
- Play Cmaj⁷ four different ways (see figure 9.3):
  1. Root Position: Place the ring finger on the root of the chord in triad seventh—root form.
  2. First Inversion Position: Place the ring finger on the third of the chord in triad seventh—first inversion form.
  3. Second Inversion Position: Place the ring finger on the fifth of the chord in triad seventh—second inversion form.
  4. Third Inversion Position: Place the ring finger on the seventh of the chord in triad seventh—third inversion form.
- Play the first four notes of the C major scale (see figure 9.4):
  1. Scale Position: Place the ring finger on the root of the chord in scale form.

Triad 7th-Root   Triad 7th-1st Inversion   Triad 7th-2nd Inversion   Triad 7th-3rd Inversion

FIGURE 9.3

FIGURE 9.4

Basic Exercises

The basic exercises help develop finger strength, independence, dexterity, and note precision:

1. Chords. Chord exercises consist of pulling full chords in two different ways: (1) unbroken (nonrolled) (figure 9.5a) and (2) broken (rolled) (figure 9.5b). While this exercise is only illustrated in root position, it should be practiced in all eight positions, with the right hand first and then the left hand.
2. Arpeggios. Arpeggio study develops individual finger strength and dexterity. Again, these exercises should be practiced in all eight positions. Remember to play very slowly and maintain a relaxed hand:
   - Ascending Arpeggio. There are two modes of performance (figure 9.6):

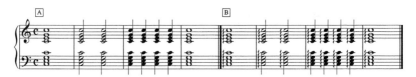

FIGURE 9.5

FIGURE 9.6

A) Place fingers, play one at a time until they are all released, then replace all four fingers simultaneously.

B) Place fingers; play one at a time; replace 4 while playing 1; and replace 3, 2, and 1 simultaneously while playing 4. Again, this is analogous to a guitarist's "full plant" and "sequential plant."

- Descending Arpeggio. There are two modes of performance (figure 9.7):

  A) Place fingers, play one at a time until they are all released, then replace all four fingers simultaneously.

  B) Place fingers; play one at a time; replace 1 while playing 4; and replace 2, 3, and 4 simultaneously while playing 1.

- Round Arpeggio. Place all fingers; play one at a time; replace 2, 3, and 4 simultaneously while playing 1; and replace 3, 2, and 1 simultaneously while playing 4 (figure 9.8).

3. Scales. Practice scales using the exercises in figure 9.9.

Navigating the Harp

Once your students learn "how to drive," they must learn how to navigate through the city streets! How do students learn to weave in and out

FIGURE 9.7

FIGURE 9.8

FIGURE 9.9

of chords with the most efficiency, accuracy, and knowledge as to what chord they are playing? In order to do this, it is important that they learn what diatonic major, minor, and diminished chords can be produced on the harp. Make sure your students understand the following: I-ii-iii-IV-V-vi-viidim-I (see figure 9.10). Advanced students with a sound foundation of diatonic harmony should also study with added sevenths (also I^6): Imaj^7-ii^7-iii^7-IVmaj^7-V^7-vi^7-vii^7(b^5)-I^6 (see figure 9.11).

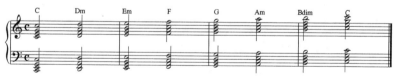

FIGURE 9.10

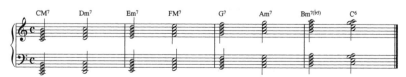

FIGURE 9.11

FIGURE 9.12

When transitioning from one chord to the next, use various positions so that far-reaching shifts are kept to a minimum. Generally speaking, you want to take the easiest route and avoid shifting in only one position because the often wide intervals between chord placements may be impractical, inefficient, and, with respect to voice leading, simply not good musical sense. Because they have so many options in selecting positions, your students should get accustomed to switching from chord to chord in different ways. Here are three suggestions for each of three common chord progressions.

1. I-V-I (see figure 9.12)
2. I-IV-V-I (see figure 9.13)
3. I-vi-ii-V-I (see figure 9.14)

Your advanced students should also modify these basic progressions to include the diatonic seventh chords. Again, three suggestions:

1. I-V^7-I (see figure 9.15)
2. I-IV-V^7-I (see figure 9.16)
3. I-vi^7-ii^7-V^7-I (see figure 9.17)

FIGURE 9.13

FIGURE 9.14

FIGURE 9.15

Bass and Chordal Accompaniment

Perhaps the greatest difficulty for harp students is acquiring right arm–left arm independence. I suggest that you kill two birds with one stone by developing this skill while simultaneously studying common mariachi rhythms. Your students' prior knowledge of basic rhythms may

FIGURE 9.16

FIGURE 9.17

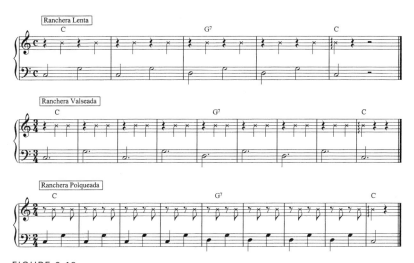

FIGURE 9.18

make it much easier for them to "tap their heads while rubbing their bellies" (see figure 9.18)! Your advanced students may then be able to execute some more difficult rhythms (see figure 9.19).

TECHNIQUES AND EFFECTS

Like few other instruments in the world, the harp has a huge variety of unique techniques and special effects that may be used to embellish your arrangements. Here are some of the most common in mariachi:

- Glissando. Slide between the two indicated notes to create a sweeping scale. The second or third finger is used to ascend while the first is used to descend (see figure 9.20).
- Tremolo. Ascend the indicated arpeggio rapidly and repeatedly (see figure 9.21).
- Arpeggio. Use both hands in three different positions to ascend and descend (see figure 9.22).

FIGURE 9.19

FIGURE 9.20

FIGURE 9.21

FIGURE 9.22

PLAYING CHROMATIC HARMONIES AND IN DIFFERENT KEYS

The technical and stylistic development of the mariachi harp has been in direct response to the musical demands of the contemporary mariachi repertoire. Essentially, harpists have developed techniques in order to cope with the drawbacks of performing polytonal music. While today the lever harp is providing a fast and efficient solution to many of the hardships caused by complex chromatic harmonies and playing in various keys, it is still a good idea to invest some time in developing compensatory techniques. When playing notes outside of the harp's diatonic tuning, you generally have three options:

1. Retune Your Harp: The most obvious solution is retuning either the entire harp or segments of the harp to the desired key. Unless you have a specific solo or important melodic passage, this may not be practical during a performance, as it is very time consuming.
2. Avoid the Note: Playing around specific notes is often an option. This method is most appropriate when performing harmonic accompaniment, as there will frequently be other voices to select from (see figure 9.23).
3. Raise the Note: Using special techniques to raise a pitch by a semitone is sometimes required, especially when performing specific bass patterns and melodic lines. Here are several common "sharping" techniques:
   - When playing bass, use the right thumb to press down on a bass string just under the tuning peg, producing the sharpened semitone when pulling that string with the left hand. Typically, you apply the sharp to the lowest octave and omit playing the upper.
   - When playing melody and harmony, use the left thumb to press down on a treble string just under the tuning peg while plucking

FIGURE 9.23

the string with the right hand. Because of the absence of bridge pins, this technique only works with mariachi harps. When playing on a different style harp, use the nail of the left index finger to press up against the string at the soundboard while plucking with the right hand. You can apply sharps to two strings simultaneously by also using the middle finger.

PURCHASING HARPS
- Roberto Morales is the most renowned mariachi harp luthier in Mexico. Based in Guadalajara, Mexico, Morales, along with his son Rubén and grandson Rubén Jr., constructs harps of three different sizes and is now integrating removable legs and Salvi sharping levers.
- Brian Steeger of San Juan Bautista, California, builds various styles of Mexican harps.
- John Westling of Sandpiper Instruments in Coquille, Oregon, manufactures the "Jalisco," a thirty-eight-string harp designed by Sergio Alonso that has an integrated preamp and Loveland sharping levers.

PURCHASING STRINGS
- Guadalupe Custom Strings in Los Angeles, California, specializes in Mexican harp strings.
- Markwood Heavenly Strings in Phoenix, Oregon, and Robinson's Harp Shop in Mount Laguna, California, are two other well-known folk-harp string manufacturers.

EDUCATIONAL RESOURCES
- www.jaliscoharp.com: William Faulkner's Web page, featuring harp photographs, biographies, recordings, and lessons.
- *Mariachi Mastery—Harp*: by Jeff Nevin and published by Kjos Music Company, is part of an entire classroom set for mariachi ensemble.

HARP TEACHERS
Nothing beats the benefit of one-on-one instruction from an experienced harpist; some notable ones appear in the following list. Several

mariachi conferences also include harp instruction in the workshop curriculum, including the Tucson International Mariachi Conference, San Jose International Mariachi Festival, *Encuentro Internacional del Mariachi y la Charrería* (Guadalajara), and Albuquerque Mariachi Spectacular Conference:

- Art Gerst: Carson, CA
- William Faulkner: Carmel, CA
- Santiago Maldonado: Fontana, CA
- Juan Morales: Wasco, CA
- Guillermo Acuña: Van Nuys, CA
- Omar López: El Paso, TX
- Alfonso García: San Fernando, CA
- Adrián Pérez: El Paso, TX
- Nicolás Alanís: McAllen, TX
- Juan Cabrera: San Antonio, TX
- Adam Romo: Las Vegas, NV
- Jesús Galicia: Fresno, CA
- Javier Rodríguez: Dallas, TX
- Ernie Ferra: Phoenix, AZ
- Sergio Alonso: Sylmar, CA

LISTENING TO THE HARP

One way to become familiar with the mariachi harp sound is by listening to some of the tradition's most recognized harpists. While many mariachi recordings do not include the harp, there are still plenty of recordings to select from:

- Andrés Huesca is Mexico's most renowned harpist and was the first to popularize the Mexican harp, especially in the *jarocho* and *ranchera* styles. He is showcased on various tribute albums, *Homenaje a Andrés Huesca,* and *Recordando a Andrés Huesca,* and appears in numerous films, including the classics *Allá en el Rancho Grande, Los Tres Huastecos,* and *Historia de Un Gran Amor.*

- Benito Martínez is perhaps the most recognized mariachi harpist, having great success as a studio musician. He appears on recordings accompanying numerous artists, including Javier Solís, Antonio Aguilar, Los Dos Oros, and Dueto América.
- Arturo Mendoza, legendary harpist of the world-renowned Mariachi Vargas de Tecalitlán, worked on countless recordings throughout his fifty-year career, accompanying artists such as David Zaízar and Cuco Sánchez.
- Antonio Maciel is credited with being the first to integrate regional Mexican harp music into mariachi. You may hear his mariachi renditions of Veracruz harp music with Mariachi México de Pepe Villa on various LPs.

In recent years, some of the world's most renowned ensembles have included harp in their studio recordings. Look for CDs of Mariachi Vargas de Tecalitlán, Mariachi Los Camperos de Nati Cano, Mariachi Nuevo Tecalitlán, Mariachi América de Jesús Rodríguez de Híjar, and Mariachi Sol de México de José Hernández.

CONCLUSION

In the process of modernization, the mariachi culture has generally excluded the harp. Despite its current marginalized role, the mariachi harp has the potential and versatility to hold a central and indispensable place in the mariachi ensemble. Reintroducing the harp traditions of the past and developing new performance techniques can give the harp a new voice in mariachi. A foundation for achieving this has been introduced in this chapter. These guidelines, of course, are only the first step in mastering an instrument that has an abundance of complexities that can take years of dedication, hard work, and perseverance to acquire. With the increased interest, energy, and commitment of students, the harp can reach the type of acceptance and prosperity it once enjoyed and still so deeply deserves.

10

Teaching Vocal Technique to Mariachi Students

Noé Sánchez

When you break a string on the violin, you can replace it. When you dent the bell of the trumpet, it can be repaired. When you damage the voice, however, it might not be so easy to correct. The human voice is a delicate instrument—it reflects the mood and well-being of the individual. Perhaps one of the most neglected instruments in the mariachi ensemble is the voice. Correct vocal technique must be part of every mariachi student's daily regimen. There is nothing worse than to see a beautifully dressed mariachi ensemble that plays with finesse only to have the vocalist ruin it for everyone listening.

Directors should take special care to incorporate vocalises (vocal warm-ups) into every rehearsal to ensure correct vocal technique. Directors should spend *at least* 5–10 minutes every day on vocal technique and incorporate these vocalises into the songs. The problem is that many mariachi directors are not trained as vocal teachers. Listening to recordings, going over the song texts, and singing the song repeatedly has been the norm in many mariachi programs across the country. Mariachi instructors should be aware that specific vocalises exist that are designed

145

to expand vocal technique, allowing our singers to perform the mariachi repertoire correctly. These vocalises reinforce certain principles of singing that every vocalist should know. Whether you sing opera, pop, or mariachi music, these principles are the same and should be taught to every singer.

THE BASIC PRINCIPLES OF SINGING

Principle 1: Posture

The student should stand up straight, one foot slightly in front of the other (shoulder width apart), shoulders back and relaxed, knees slightly bent (not locked), and head straight (chin parallel to the floor). This ensures that the body is aligned and in correct position for optimal performance.

Principle 2: Breathing

When the student breathes, the lungs should expand fully without raising the shoulders. Perhaps the best exercise for developing breathing is swimming. Swimming strengthens the muscles that help singers to sustain long notes. A good visual example for students is to have them lie on the floor face up and place a book on top of their abdomen. The only thing that moves should be the book going up and down. This type of breathing should also take place when they are standing.

Principle 3: Dropping the Jaw

To help students drop the jaw properly, encourage them to imagine that they are yawning while having an imaginary small apple inside their mouth. The tongue should be placed on the inside touching the bottom teeth when holding a long note. Vowels should be tall (north and south), not wide (east and west). Raising the soft palate is also necessary. The soft palate is toward the back of the mouth where the tissue becomes soft. By smiling and raising the eyebrows, the soft palate can be raised. These same muscles are connected to the soft palate. Many vocal problems can be corrected very quickly by applying this principle.

Principle 4: Developmental Vocalises

When warm-ups are taught, each one should have a specific purpose. These should include but are not limited to register blends (low, chest, head), scale passages for intonation and range expansion, agility exercises for fast vocal passages, vowel modification (to help through the *passaggio*), resonance exercises (for a rounder sound), *mesa di voce* for shifting from chest to head voice, arpeggios, and falsetto exercises (for expanding the male voice and teaching falsetto in *huapangos*). *The purpose of all exercises is to improve the quality and sound of the voice throughout the entire vocal range of the student.* The student should be able to sing high and low sounds both softly and loudly while still maintaining a good voice quality. Please refer to the vocalises in this chapter for examples.

Principle 5: Relax while Singing

Tension creates a harsh sound while singing. The singer should be relaxed. Do not misinterpret "relax" as meaning "do not concentrate." On the contrary, in order to relax, students have to learn to apply all the previous principles while singing.

Principle 6: Maintain Vocal Health

If the student is sick, the voice may sound weak. Students should not be singing if they have a cold or other illness that prevents them from singing correctly. Drinking lots of water is a must for any singer since the vocal cords have to be moist in order to vibrate and produce sound. Screaming and coughing should be avoided since these actions create hoarseness. Singers should always vocalize before singing in a performance.

Principle 7: Appropriate Vocal Range and Repertoire

Women singers with high-pitched voices are usually classified as sopranos; those with low-pitched voices are called altos. Higher male voices are usually classified as tenors, and lower voices are called basses.

Selecting the proper range and songs for each singer ensures a better experience for the entire mariachi ensemble. In general, women soloists should not sing songs in the same keys as those that men would sing in. Instead, songs should be transposed to the appropriate vocal range for them. *It is important that adolescent males whose voices are undergoing the changing process should not be pushed. Perhaps solos should be avoided until more stability is found in their voices.*

Principle 8: Interpretation and Style of the Song

After vocal problems have been fixed, pronunciation, translation, style, and mood need to be addressed. Gestures, if needed, can also be worked on at this time. Improvement in the quality of the students' voices *will be apparent if these principles are put into practice.* To facilitate teaching these concepts, especially the vocalises, the director should have a piano in the room. During each practice session, every vocalise should be performed, in sequence (refer to those included in this chapter). With the exception of number 1, the vocalises should be played on the piano in two octaves using both hands. They can be played chromatically up for about a fifth, depending if you are teaching middle school or high school students. You may also choose to go downward to expand the low range.

When interpreting songs, one must think of the lyrics as poetry. Translating the lyrics and understanding the poetry is crucial for interpreting songs. Sometimes we don't always think of a song as a poem, but indeed, some of the best poetry written today appears as song lyrics. This certainly includes mariachi songs. While some instructors may limit themselves to teaching the notes without teaching the meaning of the song, a thorough understanding of the lyrics completes the total picture of preparing a song for performance, along with singing the notes in tune, singing the rhythms correctly, and using good diction. Later, gestures can be added to the performance based on the lyrics.

TEACHING WITH VOCALISES

The vocalises included here (see figure 10.1 at the end of this chapter for the eleven exercises referred to here) were created by prominent voice teachers and performers, such as Manuel García II (1805–1906); John Wilcox; Alan Lingquest (1891–1984); Enrico Caruso, the great tenor (1873–1921); Mathilde Marchesi, the great soprano (1821–1913); and Virginia Botkin (1925–2002). This is not to suggest that these are the only vocalises, but these are the ones that emphasize all the principles stated earlier.

Here is a brief explanation of vocal pedagogy terminology. The vocal cords, or folds, are located in the Adam's apple. When they touch and vibrate, they produce sound (phonation). This happens when we talk or sing. When we breathe, the vocal cords are apart; when we talk or sing, they touch. In the voice, there are three acceptable vocal registers: low, chest, and head (also referred to as low, middle, and upper register, respectively). In males, there is usually a break in the voice from chest to head register. The space between the chest and head register is normally referred to as the *passaggio*.

Exercise 1: Stretching the Vocal Cords

At the beginning of every warm-up, a student should start with a lazy yawn to stretch out the vocal cords. Exercise 1 provides a demonstration of this technique. Throughout these vocalises, the student practices and applies breath management. Most of these vocalises are usually performed in one breath before moving up or down chromatically.

Exercise 2: Blending Registers and Using Falsetto

Wilcox and Lingquest recommend that students blend the upper register to the lower register by keeping the falsetto (in males) as far down as possible without hearing a break through the *passaggio*. Exercise 2 provides a demonstration of this technique. The *passaggio* is the place in the voice where a shift in mechanism has to occur in order to create higher sounds. It is also where males feel constricted or the Adam's apple begins to tighten while ascending. The challenge of this exercise is to blend the falsetto with the chest voice without breaking. Falsetto becomes stronger as proper muscles are strengthened. This helps smooth the break between the chest register into the head register. Many tenors are trained in this fashion. For mariachi purposes, this vocalise helps develop the proper singing technique for falsetto in *huapangos*.

Exercises 3, 4, and 5: Recognizing Correct Pitch and Intonation

Scale passages help students recognize and correct pitch and intonation. Exercises 3, 4, and 5 demonstrate this concept. Lingquest provided Italian syllables *nie ri tu mi kia nia bella* to introduce vowels. Another applicable method is to use the Kodály syllables *do ti la sol fa mi re do*. When a student ascends the scale and approaches his or her *passaggio*, vowel modification needs to be practiced. Vowel modification means that a singer will go from an open vowel to a closed vowel (the sequence *a, e, i, o, u* exemplifies going from an open to a closed vowel). An example of this concept is when you start a vocalise with an *a* vowel, and as you move higher into the *passaggio*, it closes and changes to an *o* vowel. Exercise 5 must be performed in this manner.

Exercise 6: Executing Fast-Moving Notes

Agility in singing is often ignored by mariachi teachers. A time will come when fast-moving notes are required, and the singer should be prepared to execute them. Proper technique can be built by using exercise 6, created by Mathilde Marchesi.

Exercises 7 and 8: Achieving Vowel Unity

Vowel unity is extremely important. Open vowels in Spanish or Italian are the best to use when practicing vocalises. Exercises 7 and 8 should be practiced with the mouth left as open as possible, making the vowel changes inside the mouth. Once a student understands this concept, then vowel changes can be practiced by using the lips. When singing, consonants should be executed as quickly as possible, thus leaving most of the sound to a vowel.

Exercise 9: Creating a Focused and Resonant Sound

Many singers have no intonation problems but have a thin sound. In order to create a more focused and resonant sound, exercise number 9 can be applied. This exercise adds nasal sounds to the existing vocal sound. My voice teacher, Virginia Botkin, introduced me to a visual metaphor for this concept. She stated that there are two types of sounds in singers: a singer with a thin sound seems to sing as if wearing a plain necklace, but when a singer adds resonance, it is as if the singer has added pearls to the necklace. The result is a more refined, focused, and pleasant sound.

A word of caution: This exercise gradually increases vocal resonance, which is sometimes confused with vibrato. The latter will occur naturally when the voice has resonance. Unfortunately, many vocal teachers try to teach vibrato to their students, who, through time, develop a rather harsh, unpleasant wobble. Students should be taught focus and resonance, not vibrato, which will gradually emerge through time as they continue to develop their vocal technique.

Exercise 10: Employing the *Mesa di Voce*

One of the world's most prominent vocal teachers was Manual García II. García developed many of today's vocal technique practices, including the use of the laryngeal mirror. He was the first to see the vocal cords using this invention. Exercise 10, the *mesa di voce* exercise, is one of the most difficult vocalises yet one of the most helpful for vocal development. The exercise was used well before García. His specific contribution was to blend all three registers, from the softest to the loudest sounds and from the lowest to highest ranges. This vocalise should be performed with full control of breath, resonance, and support from beginning to end. This is one of the most widely used vocalises in all of the opera world.

Exercise 11: Building Interval Skips with Arpeggios

The last vocalise was introduced to me by Virginia Botkin. The arpeggio, exercise 11, is crucial in building interval skips in tune. The word *aleluya* puts the concept of vowel modification into practice. The challenge of moving from note to note in large intervals of a third or more, not step by step, occurs in many mariachi songs.

Applying the concepts taught in the vocalises to the songs is crucial to developing vocal technique. Do not vocalize perfectly and then sing the song without any application of what you have learned. All eight principles mentioned earlier should be applied to the song being learned. Remember to ask yourself "What is this vocalise going to improve?" before introducing a new vocalise into your warm-up. Everything taught should have a purpose.

APPLYING VOCAL TECHNIQUE

Perhaps the best way to improve students' vocal technique is to provide individual voice lessons. Unfortunately, this is not possible in most classroom scenarios, so have the entire class stand and vocalize together. Sing the vocalises ascending and descending chromatically, thus building the voice ranges for all students. Notating all vocals completely is crucial so that students apply knowledge of musical concepts when singing. Giving students only the lyrics to a song without music notation should be discouraged. Special time should be taken to at least audition students to hear their strong and weak points as well as to classify their ranges. This is crucial in choosing appropriate repertoire for your mariachi.

Female singers should have songs transposed to their appropriate ranges. When performing duets or trios, make sure the voices are blended appropriately according to the vocal quality of the singers. Out-of-range singing makes some voices naturally louder than the others.

Special consideration should be applied when selecting soloists placed in these situations.

Listening to recordings of many different singers will improve the listening skills of your vocalists. Attending and performing in concerts will improve their stage presence and help them overcome stage fright. Recording students will provide both teachers and students with a tool for evaluating progress and pinpointing problem areas. I have found it beneficial to have *armonía* players learn to perform the vocal parts before trying to play and sing at the same time.

Words of encouragement should follow all vocal sessions. Students tend to learn at different paces. Explain that if they want to become good singers, they must exercise their voices as much as they practice their instruments. Vocal health should be part of their daily regimen. Again, students should avoid screaming and coughing and should drink plenty of water every day. If it hurts to sing, they are probably not singing correctly. They should stop and have complete vocal rest, or if they are ill, they should consult a laryngologist.

The principles of vocal technique must be put into practice every day. *These concepts and principles will only improve singing if they are consistently used in the classroom.* Do not vocalize once a week, pass out a song, and expect great results. This is not just going to happen. It is the responsibility of the director to provide students with the tools necessary to improve vocal technique and encourage them to hone them on a consistent basis. Once this practice is established, results will gradually become noticeable.

It is crucial to the development of vocal technique that students not try to imitate other singers, especially those in recordings. Everyone is different, and through conscientious vocal training, the individual voice will start to develop. Singing, without intonation problems, is expected of all students. It is what vocalists do with their technique that makes them better performers. Refer to the vocal warm-ups provided in figure 10.1.

Vocal Warm-ups
(Vocalises)

Noé Sánchez
©1995

FIGURE 10.1

VOCAL TECHNIQUE CHECKLIST
This vocal checklist will provide you with some guidance when teaching voice:

- Posture
- Breathing
- Warm-up (Vocalises):
  - Sirens/yawns
  - Register blends from high to low/falsetto
  - Scale passages for intonation
  - Agility exercises of the voice
  - Vowel unity
  - Resonance
  - *Mesa di voce*
  - Arpeggios
- Auditioning students for vocal range
- Selecting appropriate songs for singers/male versus female keys
- The male changing voice
- Listening to recordings and performances
- Recording students
- Vocal health—water, exercise, rest
- The importance of regular practice in school and at home
- Relaxing while singing
- Applying vocalises to your songs
- The importance of notating the song
- Singing and playing at the same time (*armonía* section)

BIBLIOGRAPHY
Coffin, B. (1987). *Coffin's sounds of singing* (2nd ed). Metuchen, NJ: Scarecrow Press.

Garcia, M. (1894, 1982). *Hints on singing*. New York: Joseph Patelson Music House.

Mathis, B. (1990). Selected vocal exercises and their relationship to specific laryngeal conditions: A description of seven case studies. (Ph.D. dissertation, University of North Texas at Denton, 1990). *University Microfilms International.*

Miller, R. (1986). *The structure of singing.* New York: Shirmer Books.

VanManen, A. (1978). *Falsetto.* Springfield, MO: Temple Press.

Vennard, W. (1967). *Singing: The mechanism and the technic.* New York: Carl Fischer.

11

Mariachi Education as a District Initiative

Development of the Clark County School District Program

JAVIER TRUJILLO AND MARCIA NEEL

As the Clark County School District (CCSD) of Las Vegas, Nevada, approached the millennium, its student population continued to rise at a staggering rate from 121,918 in 1990 to 231,125 in 2000—nearly 110,000 students in 10 years (these and all figures are from the CCSD Student Data Services). The music program had continued to grow side by side with the increase in student population, so to broaden the course offerings, the CCSD implemented a guitar curriculum in the late 1990s. By 2000, the district had become the sixth largest in the country. The increase in the Latino population exceeded all others proportionately, and because the CCSD music program is always looking to serve its students, the mariachi program was the natural next step in the evolution of a comprehensive curriculum. The CCSD subsequently established the Secondary Mariachi Education Program in the summer of 2002 with the aim of providing:

- Increased student enrollment in music education courses
- Opportunities to represent the CCSD and the Las Vegas community as music ambassadors through high-level performances

- Increased academic achievement by requiring a passing GPA to participate
- Increased student attendance
- Increased parent participation
- Increased self-esteem and self-confidence
- Positive social citizenry through performances
- A strengthened and culturally diversified fine arts department focus
- Opportunities for students to serve as positive peer role models.

The program began with five full-time mariachi educators in the 2002–2003 school year. Within five years, that number grew to fifteen, and the program had an expanded list of goals, objectives, and activities.

Since the philosophy was to provide the CCSD student population with additional opportunities for music making, the development of a comprehensive mariachi program was an obvious way to serve our community. At that time, the biggest challenge seemed to be how to get started. How could we sell the program, recruit and license the appropriate educators, write a standards-based curriculum, organize new kinds of performance experiences, and provide appropriate professional development for this new program? The answers as they have evolved for the CCSD Secondary Music Education Program are presented here.

I. SELLING THE PROGRAM
One would think that selling a mariachi program in a community that reflected an increasingly larger Latino population would be easy; however, it did present a number of challenges. The superintendent, board members, upper-level administrators, and principals were anxious to develop mariachi programs, as were members of the Latino community.

The orchestra and band directors were more cautious for all of the obvious reasons: the nontraditional style of music that would be taught, the concern that students would not be approaching music academically through music literacy, and the primary fear that the mariachi program would detract from the programs already in place. It was thus determined that of the forty-five middle schools and thirty-four high schools in the district, the mariachi program would be piloted in only six secondary schools. This decision alleviated much of the concern on the part of the instrumental educators, allowing the program to develop in a methodical manner based on the recommendation of the professional mariachi musicians who would oversee its implementation.

II. RECRUITING MARIACHI EDUCATORS

Once the CCSD decided to implement a mariachi program, the next task was to find the educators who could ensure its success. One of the members of the CCSD board of school trustees knew of a program at Pueblo High School in Tucson, Arizona, which was one of the better-known, curriculum-based programs. Rather than visiting Pueblo High School, the CCSD invited the Pueblo High School Mariachi Aztlán ensemble to Las Vegas for a week of performing assemblies in the recommended pilot schools to see how the genre would be received. In addition, the school's assistant principal, Richard Carranza—a former mariachi educator himself—came to Las Vegas to present a workshop for CCSD music educators who already had an interest in this genre. The feedback from the assemblies and workshops was extremely positive, leaving the district administration confident that a mariachi program would indeed be successful and supported by students.

As is the case with all fields in music education, finding the best teachers is the surest way to guarantee the success of a program. With that in mind, the CCSD hired Javier Trujillo, who had been serving as the director of Mariachi Aztlán at Pueblo High School in Tucson. Four other mariachi musicians were hired to serve as teachers in the first year. Javier's schedule allowed him to split his time between teaching and serving as a program facilitator. In this way, he could visit with the four other mariachi educators on a regular basis to ensure consistency in delivering instruction.

III. LICENSING MARIACHI EDUCATORS

Early in the process of developing the program's philosophy, the district realized that because mariachi education is not a teacher preparation major offered at the university level, the best mariachi educators would have to come from the performance industry. Since all music educators in Nevada are required to possess a music education license, this presented a real challenge.

In a meeting with the assistant superintendent, the CCSD decided to request that the state department of education endorse mariachi within the business and industry (B&I) category of teacher licensing. The B&I category is used when licensing professionals from the business world to work within the school district. Thus, the prospective mariachi educators would leave their professional mariachi performance careers to introduce the program into the schools. To qualify for this license, these teachers would need at least three years' successful performance experience in a professional mariachi ensemble.

IV. ESTABLISHING A SEQUENTIAL CURRICULUM BASED ON THE CONTENT STANDARDS

The CCSD implemented the Secondary Mariachi Education Program with the objective of providing students of various ethnicities with an exceptional educational experience that would expand their cultural awareness and promote a lifelong appreciation for music. The students, many of them from lower socioeconomic backgrounds, would be offered a high-quality musical experience of a traditional music form through a program organized around a sound, sequential, standards-based curriculum. Additionally, students would develop sensitivity, understanding, and respect for peoples from a broad spectrum of ethnic-cultural backgrounds. The following are the goals, objectives, activities, and materials and equipment standards of the CCSD Secondary Mariachi Education Program.

Goals

- Students will gain an understanding of the historical development of mariachi music.
- Students will explore and experiment with different musical styles and techniques to further their understanding of improvisation and musical interpretation.
- Students will gain confidence in their abilities as individual musicians and as members of a group.
- Students will participate in high-quality musical experiences from an established musical tradition.
- Students will gain an understanding of musical form.
- Students will gain and develop a lifelong appreciation of and interest in music.
- Students will develop critical-thinking and problem-solving skills and a sense of personal responsibility as they increase their performance skills.

Objectives

- To develop an appreciation for musical form and its development
- To understand regional and historical variations of mariachi music
- To develop the ability to successfully demonstrate a variety of mariachi skills and techniques using appropriate instruments
- To incorporate traditional rhythms used in mariachi music into musical performances
- To increase awareness of the literal and emotional content of music

Activities

The implementation of a comprehensive mariachi education curriculum includes the following steps:

- The development of appropriate course syllabi
- The enhancement of equipment standards (instruments) at each school site
- The presentation of professional development for the mariachi faculty

In order to meet these goals and objectives, the CCSD formed the Mariachi Curriculum-Writing Task Force comprised of a number of mariachi educators. The primary objective of this task force was to design a sequential, standards-based curriculum outlining recommended activities for instructional purposes.

Examples of mariachi curriculum documents currently available are:

- Beginning Mariachi Guitar/*Vihuela* (available at www.menc.org/mariachi)
- Beginning Mariachi Violin (available at www.menc.org/mariachi)
- Mariachi Ensemble I (available at www.musiceducationconsultants.net)
- Mariachi Ensemble II (available at www.musiceducationconsultants.net)
- Mariachi Ensemble III (available at www.musiceducationconsultants.net)

Materials and Equipment Standards

According to the "Opportunity-to-Learn Standards for Music Instruction," published by MENC and available at www.menc.org, the equipment standards in music

> are intended to specify the physical and educational conditions necessary in the schools to enable every student, with sufficient effort, to meet the content standards in music. [While these equipment standards] focus on the learning environment necessary to teach music, it is important to note that the ultimate objective of all standards, all school curricula, and all school personnel is to help students to gain the broad skills and knowledge that will enable them to function effectively as adults and to contribute to society in today's world and tomorrow's.

The following instruments should be provided in sufficient quantity:

- Violin
- Guitar

- Trumpet
- *Guitarrón*
- *Vihuela*

At least fifteen new songs for each level of mariachi ensemble are added each year. Sufficient repertoire should be available to provide a three-year cycle of instructional material; by the end of high school, the students will have a mariachi repertoire of about fifty songs. The district's library of music for performing groups is sufficient to provide a folder of music for each student per stand. The library contains no materials produced in violation of copyright laws, as staff members provide the arrangements of songs available in the public domain, along with some original pieces. Every room in which mariachi is taught is equipped with a high-quality sound-reproduction system capable of using current recording technology. Each school should contain a library that provides audio and video mariachi materials.

V. ORGANIZING A MARIACHI FESTIVAL

The CCSD Secondary Mariachi Education Program provides an annual three-day Mariachi Conference and Festival where students from across the district participate in two days of master classes (music-making workshops) taught by renowned, professional clinicians/performers of the mariachi art form. In this setting, students learn and perform a variety of music that demonstrates the highest level of musicianship possible for their specific school size and level of experience. Clinicians who are renowned for their professional musical accomplishments provide students with two days of intensive music workshops and one day of dress rehearsals where they further develop their skills as musicians and performers. The Mariachi Conference and Festival culminates in a professional concert production in which all student participants display their musical talents and newly acquired musical skills to an audience of proud parents, school district personnel, and at-large community members.

VI. PROFESSIONAL DEVELOPMENT FOR MARIACHI EDUCATORS

While it can be assumed that students in instrumental music classes are already instructed according to Nevada's music content standard (NCS) 2 (performing on instruments) and that choral students are taught according to NCS 1 (singing), it can be difficult to "teach to the standards" on a daily basis. The CCSD is dedicated to continually improving the quality of our schools, and the Professional Development Program operates to train our staff through professional development workshops and classes.

The Professional Development Program assists mariachi educators in implementing specific teaching techniques and strategies to make NCSs a regular part of their teaching. All of the content standards are addressed through the Professional Development Program, for example:

- Singing and playing of a variety of mariachi repertoire (NCSs 1 and 2)
- Reading and notating music (NCS 5)
- Listening to, analyzing, and describing music (NCS 6)
- Evaluating music and music performances (NCS 7)
- Understanding music in relation to history and culture (NCS 9)

VII. DEVELOPMENT OF OTHER RELEVANT PERFORMANCE EXPERIENCES

Providing students with performance opportunities plays a key role in their development as musicians. More important, it reinforces the concepts and skills learned in the classroom and increases self-confidence and self-esteem in each individual performer.

The Secondary Mariachi Education Program offers the following:

- A summer mariachi institute for students,
- A districtwide holiday concert, and
- A mariachi festival (adjudicated) in the spring.

Eventually, students form their own mariachi ensembles for fun and perform in the community at all sorts of parties, including *quinceañeras*.

They remain involved in the school program, as it continues to challenge them with frequent high-visibility performances.

Within the next decade, mariachi programs are expected to explode across the country. It is hoped that the positive experiences and results that we have had in the CCSD will help music educators and districts alike as they move to implement a comprehensive mariachi curriculum in their schools.

REFERENCES

MENC: The National Association for Music Education. (1994). *Opportunity-to-learn standards for music instruction: Grades preK–12.* www.menc.org/publication/books/otl.html.

12

Mariachi Instruction in Support of Literacy

RICHARD CARRANZA

"So, how will this program help our school achieve its academic improvement goals?" This is probably one of the first questions the intrepid music educator is asked when proposing the creation of a mariachi program. Even scarier is when it is posed during an evaluation conference while discussing an existing program.

A corpus of research shows a strong correlation between music education and increased student achievement in core content areas and the development of higher-order thinking and reasoning skills. For example, a study reported in the *Journal of Research in Music Education* showed that students enrolled in high-quality music programs performed 22 percent better on English and 20 percent better on math standardized tests than students not in music programs (Johnson and Memmott, 2006).

In 2006, MENC commissioned Harris Interactive, Inc., to conduct a nationwide poll of public high school principals to assess the links between the quality of a school's music program and known educational outcome measures for the schools. The poll revealed that schools with music programs—especially those with high-quality programs—have significantly higher graduation rates and attendance rates than schools without music programs. See MENC's "Why Music Education?" page at www.menc.org/facts for more research on the benefits of music education.

The music educator must be armed with an arsenal of tools to provide literacy-based, high-yield instructional practices that engage students in the mastery of the musical content as well as the acquisition of strong literacy knowledge. A well-structured mariachi music program, like any well-structured music education program, should strongly support any school's or school district's literacy goals. With that in mind, I'd like to offer some tools for your instructional toolbox.

Literacy development is predicated upon active student participation in the processing of information and the use of writing at every opportunity. The following tools provide students with an opportunity to process information that has just been presented, viewed, or encountered through direct hands-on experience. These activities and strategies may be adapted as needed.

"3-2-1" ACTIVITY

After presenting an explanation or demonstration on the typical song form of a *canción ranchera* such as "Ella," pass out index cards and have each student list:

- Three important terms or ideas to remember;
- Two ideas or concepts they would like to know more about; and
- One concept or skill they think they have mastered.

This activity is excellent for quickly checking on student mastery and progress.

"TICKET OUT THE DOOR"

Pass out half sheets of paper five minutes before the end of class or rehearsal. Ask each student to write one concept that they learned well today and two questions that they still have or concepts that they don't yet understand. This activity is not only valuable when used as a check for understanding at the conclusion of the current lesson but when reintroduced as a review at the beginning of the next class, as well.

"A NOTE TO A FRIEND"

At the end of an explanation or demonstration, pass out paper asking each student to write a note to a friend explaining the process, concept, or rule they have just learned. For example, let's say you have just taught the beginning mariachi guitar students how to play the I–IV–V chords in the key of G major. Students would then describe, in detail, how to play a G major chord:

> To play a G major chord, you must begin by placing the first finger of your left hand on the fifth string, on the second fret. This creates the note B. The next step is to place your second finger on the sixth string, on the third fret. This creates the note G. The final step is to place your third finger on the first string, on the third fret. This creates another note G. It is very important to arch the fingers so that they don't interfere with the D, G, and B notes you will play on the open strings when you strum the chord.

Again, this is an excellent check for understanding while providing content-specific opportunities for students to engage in writing.

K-W-L GROUPS

One of the most useful tools for preparing student mariachi ensembles for performance is to watch professional mariachis "in action" on video. "K-W-L" groups are effective in preparing students to maximize the educational experience derived from viewing of videotapes, films, and even PowerPoint presentations. Before viewing, have students work in groups of three to five. You might choose to group the students by instrument section—violins, trumpets, and *armonías*. Each group is asked to compose a log, listing things they already *K*now about the subject of the video, along with what they *W*ant to know about the subject or questions they want answered. Then show the video or film to the class as a whole. Afterward, have the groups revise their logs, circling the *K*nown information that was covered, putting asterisks next to questions that were answered, and listing additional facts or concepts they *L*earned as a result of their viewing experience. Depending upon how well the *W*s and *L*s match up, the various groups' logs then form the basis for implementation of the desired lesson from the video.

CORNELL NOTES

The Cornell Note-Taking System was developed by Walter Pauk at Cornell University as an effective tool for his students to use for recalling and reviewing lecture information. In the years since its creation, Cornell Notes have become a standard format for note taking in many English language arts classrooms in the No Child Left Behind era.

The Cornell Note-Taking System uses a five-step process: record, question, recite, reflect, and review. The system structures the notes page into several segments that facilitate the note-taking and studying process. Students use the cue column (one fourth of the page's width on the left-hand side) to list key terms. Students record sentences and phrases in the note-taking column (three fourths of the page's width on the right-hand side), and they use a two-inch row across the bottom of the page to summarize the lecture after class (Pauk, 2001, p. 238–39). For a sample note-taking page, see the Cornell University's Center for Learning and Teaching Web page atwww.clt.cornell.edu/campus/learn/SSWorkshops/SKResources.html.

The Cornell Notes format provides a useful structure for note taking in the mariachi classroom—particularly when direct instruction is required. As principal, I encouraged all my teachers—*across the curriculum*—to implement this system. Teachers in certain areas, such as physical education and the arts, were initially skeptical, doubting its relevance to their subject matter. I responded by challenging them to adapt the note-taking document to fit their specialized needs. An adapted format for use in a music classroom might substitute a music staff for the note-taking

Student:_____

Period:_____ Date:_____

Topic:_____

Questions/Main Ideas

_____
_____
_____
_____
_____

_____   2
_____
_____
_____
_____

_____   3
_____
_____
_____
_____

_____   4
_____
_____
_____
_____

Summary:_____
_____
_____
_____
_____
_____

FIGURE 12.1
Created by Steven New, Eldorado High School, Las Vegas, Nevada, 2006

column, for instance (see figure 12.1). In this way, they came to feel a sense of ownership of the system, simultaneously reaping the benefits it put within the students' grasp.

Substantial research shows that questions that require students to "analyze information (higher-level questions) produce more learning than questions that simply require students to recall or recognize information (lower-order questions)" (Marzano, Pickering, and Pollock, 2001, 113–14). Bloom's taxonomy is the classic model used to classify the level of questioning from lower to higher levels: knowledge → comprehension → application → analysis → synthesis → evaluation. Devising music-related writing assignments to engage students at the higher levels of Bloom's taxonomy is a great way to incorporate literacy-based activities within the mariachi classroom. Table 12.1 shows some question starters and potential activities for each level of Bloom's taxonomy.

Table 12.1.   Question Starters and Potential Activities

Question Starters	Potential Activities
Knowledge	
What is the definition of a *ranchera valseada*?	Describe the _____.
What happens after measure _____?	Write a list of steps in _____ facts about _____.
What are the characteristics of _____?	Make a chart showing _____.
How many _____?	Play the notes in measure _____.
Tell in your own words _____.	
Comprehension	
Why are these *sones* similar?	Compare this _____ with _____.
How are these *huapangos* different?	Write a review of _____.
In your own words, retell what the lyrics of _____ tell _____.	Prepare a chart to show the sequence _____.
What are some examples _____?	Play a three-chord progression in the key of _____.
Can you provide a definition of _____?	
Application	
What is another instance of _____?	Play the passage using *son* phrasing.
Demonstrate the way to play _____.	Scan a collection of recordings of _____ to illustrate a particular aspect of the various musical arrangements.
Which one is most like _____?	
Which intervals would you change _____?	Create a short musical piece to depict _____.

Question Starters	*Potential Activities*
Analysis	
What are the three harmonic parts of _____?	Design a questionnaire about _____.
	Make a flow chart to show _____.
What steps are important in the process of performing _____?	Prepare a report about the area of study.
If _____, then _____.	Construct a chart to show the stylistic differences between *Mariachi Vargas* and _____ when playing s*ones jaliscienses.*
What is the relationship between _____ and _____?	
Synthesis	
Can you design a _____?	Create a model that shows your new ideas.
Compose a song about _____.	
Compose a *corrido* about _____.	Devise an original plan for _____.
Devise your own way to _____.	Finish the incomplete _____.
Develop a proposal for _____.	Change _____ so that it will _____.
How would you deal with _____?	Propose a method to _____.
Invent a method to _____.	Give the *ranchera*, *son, huapango* a new title.
Evaluation	
In your opinion, _____.	Prepare a list of criteria you would use to judge a _____. Indicate priority rating you would give.
Grade or rank the _____.	
What do you think the chord resolution to _____?	Conduct a debate about _____.
Which *mariachi* style do you prefer? Why?	Prepare an annotated bibliography.
	Prepare a case to present your opinions about _____.
Which is the most traditional Jalisco sound and why?	List some common assumptions about _____.
	Rationalize your reactions.
	Evaluate our recent performance at _____.

Adapted from Gregory and Chapman, *Differentiated Instructional Strategies: One Size Doesn't Fit All*, 2002.

We must remember that the mariachi classroom is, above all, a classroom. Writing at *every* opportunity is of vital importance. Compared with our colleagues in the core content areas, we mariachi teachers have perhaps the best precondition for engaging students in the writing process. Our students *really* want to be in our classes— *they have already "bought into it!"* It is my hope that the incorporation of some of the techniques presented here will help you, the mariachi teacher, to make mariachi music education an invaluable vehicle for our students to discover and express both their musical and academic voices.

BIBLIOGRAPHY

Bellanca, J., and Fogarty, R. (1990). *Blueprints for thinking in the cooperative classroom.* Palatine, IL: Skylight.

Gregory, G., and Chapman, C. (2002). *Differentiated instructional strategies: One size doesn't fit all.* Thousand Oaks, CA: Corwin Press.

Harmin, M. (1994). *Inspiring active learning: A handbook for teachers.* Alexandria, VA: Association for Supervision and Curriculum Development.

Harris Interactive, Inc. (2006). *Understanding the linkages between music education and educational outcomes.* Rochester, NY: Harris Interactive.

Johnson, C. M., and Memmott, J. E. (2006). Examination of relationship between participation in school music programs of differing quality and standardized test results. *Journal of Research in Music Education, 54* (4), 293–307.

Kagan, S. (1990). *Cooperative learning: Resources for teachers.* San Juan Capistrano, CA: Resources for Teachers.

Marzano, R., Pickering, D., and Pollock, J. (2001). *Classroom instruction that works.* Alexandria, VA: Association for Supervision and Curriculum Development.

Pauk, W. (2001). *How to study in college* (7th ed). Boston, MA: Houghton Mifflin.

Saphier, J., and Haley, M. (1993a). *Activators: Activity structures to engage students' thinking before instruction.* Carlisle, MA: Research for Better Teaching.

Saphier, J., and Haley, M. (1993b). *Summarizers: Activity structures to support integration and retention of new learning.* Carlisle, MA: Research for Better Teaching.

Appendix

Songs a Mariachi Student Should Know

Compiled by the MENC National Mariachi Advisory Committee

Boleros	Amor Eterno (Juan Gabriel)
	Bésame Mucho (Consuelo Velásquez)
	Cerca Del Mar (Ezequiel Cisneros Cárdenas)
	Cien Años (Rubén Fuentes, Alberto Cervantes)
	De Qué Manera te Olvido (Federico Méndez)
	Gema (Güicho Cisneros)
	Llorarás (Rafael Ramírez)
	Ojos Españoles (Bert Kaempfert)
	Por Mujeres Como Tú (Enrique Guzmán Yáñez)
	El Reloj (Roberto Cantoral)
	Sabor a Mí (Alvaro Carrillo)
	Si Nos Dejan (José Alfredo Jiménez)
	Sin Ti (Pepe Guízar)
	Solamente una Vez (Agustín Lara)
	Somos Novios (Armando Manzanero)
	Tú Me Acostumbraste (F. Domínguez)
Chotis	La Barca de Oro
	Las Golondrinas (Narciso Serradell)

Corridos	El Caballo Blanco (José Alfredo Jiménez)
	Carabina Treinta Treinta (Genaro Núñez)
	Siete Leguas (Graciela Olmos)
Cumbias	El Camaron Pelao (Valentín Elizalde)
	El Mariachi Loco (Román Palomar)
Danzones	Como Quién Pierde una Estrella (Humberto Estrada)
	Juárez (Esteban Alfonso)
	Nereidas (Amador Pérez "Dimas")
Huapangos	Cielo Rojo (Juan Zaízar)
	Cucurrucucú, Paloma (Tomás Méndez Sosa)
	Dos Arbolitos (Chucho Martínez Gil)
	El Jinete (José Alfredo Jiménez)
	La Malagueña (Elpidio Ramírez, Pedro Galindo)
	Serenata Huasteca (José Alfredo Jiménez)
Jarabes	La Botella (Felipe Bermejo)
	El Jarabe Tapatío (Felipe Alonso Partichela)
	La Raspa (Nacho García)
Joropos	Alma Llanera (Pedro Elías Gutiérrez)
	La Bikina (Alejandro F. Roth)
	La Fuente (Jesús Rodríguez de Híjar, Rigoberto Alfaro)
	La Gruta (Jesús Rodríguez de Híjar, Rigoberto Alfaro)
	Mi Ciudad (Guadalupe Trigo)
Marchas	Zacatecas (Genaro Codina)
Pasodobles	El Dos Negro (Encarnación D. Anaya)
	España Cañí (Pascual Marquina)
	El Niño Perdido (Ramón Márquez)
	El Zopilote Mojado (Zenón H. Flores)
Polkas	Café Colón (Miguel Martínez)
	Las Coronelas (Bonifacio Collazos)

	Bailando Garabato
	Jesusita en Chihuahua (Quirino Mendoza y Cortés)
	Los Machetes (Miguel Martínez)
	Las Perlitas (Francisco Cárdenas)
Potpourrís	Allá en el Rancho
	Mis Caballos
	Que Viva Veracruz II (Pepe Martínez, Agustín Lara, Lorenzo Barcelata)
	Veracruz III
	Viva Veracruz (arr. Pepe Martínez)
Rancheras	La Adelita
	Allá en el Rancho Grande (Emilio D. Uranga, Juan Días del Moral)
	Ay, Jalisco No Te Rajes (Manuel Esperón, Ernesto Cortázar)
	La Cama de Piedra (Cuco Sánchez)
	Camino de Guanajuato (José Alfredo Jiménez)
	Caminos de Michoacán (Bulmaro Bermúdez)
	Canción Mixteca (José López Alavés)
	Cielito Lindo (Quirino Mendoza y Cortés)
	Ella (José Alfredo Jiménez)
	El Herradero (Pedro Galindo)
	Los Laureles
	La Ley del Monte (José Angel Espinosa— "Ferrusquilla")
	Las Mañanitas
	México Lindo y Querido (Chucho Monge)
	Paloma Negra (Tomás Méndez Sosa)
	Por un Amor (Gilberto Parra)
	El Rey (José Alfredo Jiménez)
	Tú, Sólo Tú (Felipe Valdez Leal)
	Volver, Volver (Fernando Z. Maldonado)

Sones Jaliscienses	Las Abajeñas
	El Caballito (Manuel S. Acuña)
	El Carretero
	Las Copetonas
	La Culebra
	Guadalajara (Pepe Guízar)
	La Madrugada
	El Maracumbé
	La Negra
	El Perico Loro
	El Riflero
Sones Jarochos	El Cascabel
	La Bamba
Valses	Alejandra (Enrique Mora)
	Aniversario (Ivanovici)
	Dios Nunca Muere (Macedonio Alcalá)
	Olímpica (José Herrera)
	Sentimiento (Jesús Alcaraz)
	Viva Mi Desgracia (Francisco Cárdenas)

About the Contributors

Sergio "Checo" Alonso received his bachelor's degree in ethnomusicology from the University of California, Los Angeles, and a master's degree in education from National University. Checo teaches music at San Fernando High School and directs the school's student mariachi ensemble, Mariachi Los Tigres. He is also an instructor for the award-winning youth arts education program Mariachi Master Apprentice Program, serves as vice chair for the Cultural Arts Commission for the city of San Fernando, and is the harpist for the world-renowned Mariachi Los Camperos de Nati Cano.

©Robert Pancheco

Richard Carranza is the superintendent of the Northwest Region in the Clark County School District located in Las Vegas, Nevada. While principal of Eldorado High School in Las Vegas, he has overseen a decrease in the school's dropout rate and increase in the percent of students meeting or exceeding the state's proficiency requirements in English/language arts and math. He earned an M.Ed. in educational leadership from Northern Arizona University in Flagstaff and is currently working on his Ed.D. from the same university.

Steve Carrillo of Tucson, Arizona, has been playing mariachi music for forty years. He is the musical director of Mariachi Cobre, which he started in 1971 with his brother Randy. He was also a member of the first U.S. mariachi *juvenil*, "Los Changuitos Feos."

Mark Fogelquist received his M.A. from the University of California, Los Angeles, in 1975 and for twenty years directed Mariachi Uclatlán, a professional ensemble that appeared at numerous mariachi festivals and shared the stage with the top echelon of mariachis. He began Washington State's first school mariachi program and developed Mariachi Northwest, a five-day mariachi conference. In 2001, he returned to California to teach mariachi and estab-lished an award-award-winning student mariachi (Mariachi Chula Vista) and a highly respected mariachi conference (the Viejas-Sweetwater Mariachi Conference).

William Gradante was born and raised in the multiethnic community known as the "South End" of Hartford, Connecticut. He earned his B.A. in music at Middlebury College in Vermont, where he graduated magna cum laude and was a Phi Beta Kappa scholar. Under the guidance of ethnomusicologist Ronald Smith, Gradante spent six months doing ethnomusicological research in a small town in the southern Colombian Andes, resulting in a three-hundred-page B.A. thesis. He did his graduate work at the University of Texas at Austin, where he studied with some of the most respected folklorists and ethnomusicologists of the day. During this time, the "dean of Latin American folklorists," the venerable Américo Paredes, introduced Gradante to mariachi music. After three more research trips to Colombia and ten years in the stacks at the Institute of Latin American Studies, Gradante produced an 850-page doctoral dissertation on Colombian folk musical improvisation and had begun a lifelong love affair with mariachi music.

Gradante has spent the last twenty-eight years teaching mariachi classes at J. P. Elder Middle School and North Side High School, while spending weekends as a professional mariachi. He has published academic articles on the music of José Alfredo Jiménez, Colombian folk music, and low-rider culture.

A veteran of thirty-six years in public school music education, **Marcia Neel** served as the supervisor of the Secondary Music Education Program of the Clark County School District in Las Vegas, Nevada, from 1994 through 2007. Under her leadership, the secondary program grew to three hundred secondary music educators teaching an enrollment of over fifty thousand in fifty-six middle schools and thirty-eight high schools. Marcia is now president of Music Education Consultants, Inc., and serves as a consultant on a variety of music education projects, including the publication of a series of mariachi method books.

Mack Ruiz is a founding member of world-renowned Mariachi Cobre and has been a part of the Orlando, Florida–based Walt Disney World Entertainment along with other founding members of Cobre for twenty-six years, performing at Epcot and promoting music education nationwide. He is the educational coordinator for the Las Cruces International Mariachi Conference.

Noé Sánchez has a bachelor's degree in music education and a master's degree in musicology/ethnomusicology with a specialization in Latin American music. He has started seven mariachi programs, published choral and mariachi music, and provided mariachi curriculum guides for schools starting mariachi programs. He is a coauthor of the teacher edition of *Mariachi Mastery*, the first mariachi method book published by a major publishing company (Kjos).

Javier Trujillo has been a member of the world-renowned Mariachi Cobre, playing the *guitarra de golpe* and other instruments. He now oversees the mariachi programs in Clark County, Las Vegas. Clark County has one of America's largest music education programs, and its mariachi program is a model for others around the country.

John A. Vela is in his eighth year as director of bands at San Diego Independent School District in San Diego, Texas, and has performed as a professional mariachi musician for thirty years. He has been a music educator for the past twenty-six years. He has published numerous mariachi arrangements, instructional videos, and a beginner *guitarrón* book.